WHAT'S
WRONG with
MY HORSE?

COLIN J. VOGEL
BVetMed, MRCVS

DAVID & CHARLES

Cover photographs: (top) Bob Langrish;
(below) Derek Croucher

A catalogue record for this book is available from the British Library.

ISBN 0 7153 0489 5

Line illustrations by Jennifer Johnson unless otherwise specified,
based on material by Colin J. Vogel
Illustration on p1 by Joy Claxton

© Text: Colin J. Vogel, 1990, 1996

First published 1990
Reprinted 1991, 1992, 1993, 1994
New edition in paperback 1996

Typeset by ABM Typographics Limited, Hull
and printed in Great Britain by Redwood Books,
Trowbridge, Wiltshire
for David & Charles plc
Brunel House   Newton Abbot   Devon

Contents

Contents

Introduction

The purpose of this introduction is to help you to make the best use of the book. You will find that each chapter follows a common format. Under each chapter heading is a diagram of a horse. On this are indicated the common sites of problems which involve the particular body system being discussed. If the problem affects the body as a whole, rather than a specific part of the body, then that condition is listed under the 'General' heading. An example of this might be anaemia, which obviously affects the whole body because the blood supply is for the whole body. After this diagram a few general paragraphs follow about the horse's anatomy, so that when individual conditions are discussed you will be able to understand their effect on the horse and its performance. Finally the common, everyday, problems which may affect the horse are dealt with in more detail.

I would stress that this book is not a comprehensive list of every veterinary problem in the horse. For such detail you should consult *The Horse's Health from A to Z* (David & Charles new edn., 1989). The conditions discussed in this book are either ones which are frequently diagnosed by owners without even needing to consult a veterinary surgeon, or they are conditions which are so common that every horse-owner should have some knowledge of them, and some idea as to any immediate treatment they may need. In this respect, I have included a clearly marked ACTION section for each condition. In this the most important first aid measures are printed in **bold** type so that at a glance in an emergency you can see what constitutes first aid for that particular problem.

Disease is any variation from the normal. It follows that before you can recognise disease, you must be able to recognise normality. The normal signs of health for any individual

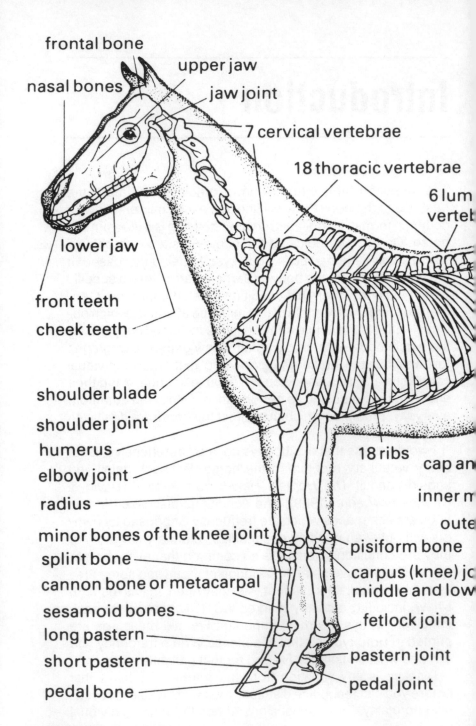

frontal bone
nasal bones
upper jaw
jaw joint
7 cervical vertebrae
18 thoracic vertebrae
6 lum
verteb
lower jaw
front teeth
cheek teeth
shoulder blade
shoulder joint
humerus
elbow joint
radius
minor bones of the knee joint
splint bone
cannon bone or metacarpal
sesamoid bones
long pastern
short pastern
pedal bone
18 ribs
cap an
inner m
oute
pisiform bone
carpus (knee) jo
middle and low
fetlock joint
pastern joint
pedal joint

The Horse's Skeleton

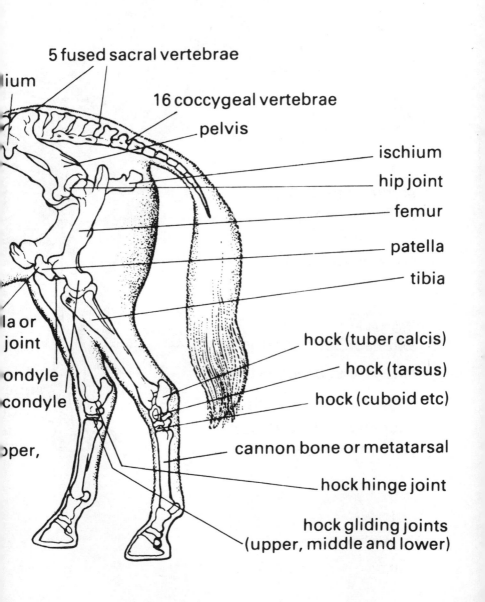

5 fused sacral vertebrae

ilium

16 coccygeal vertebrae

pelvis

ischium

hip joint

femur

patella

tibia

la or
joint

ondyle

condyle

hock (tuber calcis)

hock (tarsus)

hock (cuboid etc)

per,

cannon bone or metatarsal

hock hinge joint

hock gliding joints
(upper, middle and lower)

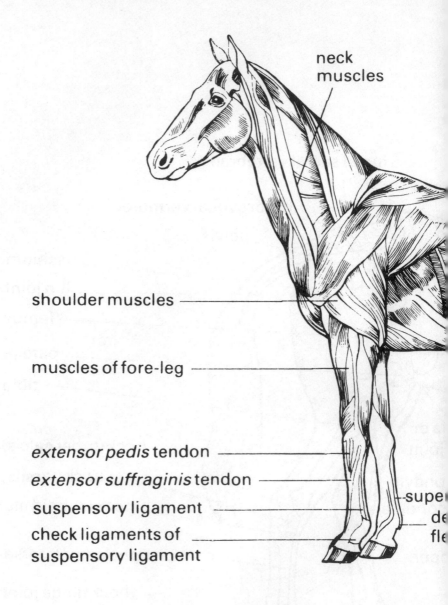

neck
muscles

shoulder muscles

muscles of fore-leg

extensor pedis tendon

extensor suffraginis tendon

suspensory ligament

check ligaments of
suspensory ligament

supe

de
fle

The Muscles of the Horse

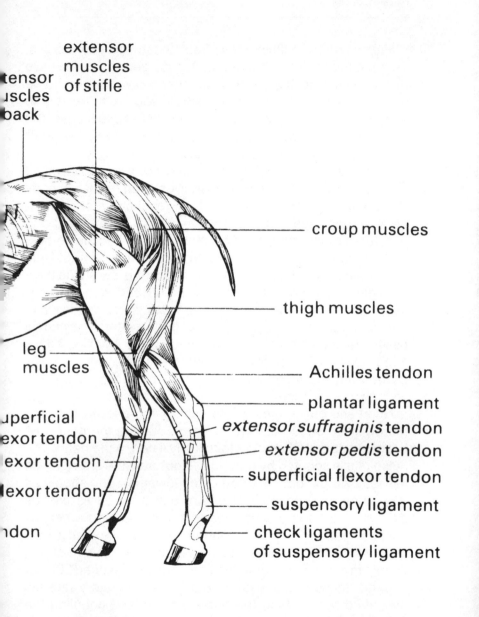

extensor
muscles
of stifle

tensor
uscles
back

croup muscles

thigh muscles

leg
muscles

Achilles tendon

plantar ligament

extensor suffraginis tendon

extensor pedis tendon

uperficial
exor tendon

superficial flexor tendon

exor tendon

suspensory ligament

lexor tendon

check ligaments
of suspensory ligament

ndon

horse may vary considerably from those of other horses. Temperament, size and breed, for instance, can all have marked effects in this regard. You must know your own horse or horses like the back of your hand if you are to be able to spot the very first signs of disease. In almost every case, the earlier you diagnose a disease and start treatment, the better your chances of a successful cure.

There are five main signs of health which it is reasonable to expect an owner to be able to assess on a regular basis: body temperature, heart or pulse rate, respiratory rate, temperament and feeding pattern. The horse's temperature is measured by inserting a clinical thermometer into the horse's rectum, and leaving it to 'incubate' for about a minute. Hold the tail steady during this time so that it cannot swish the thermometer out onto the floor, and if you can also hold the thermometer in case the horse passes some faeces and pushes it out that way then so much the better. The normal healthy temperature is about 101°F (38.3°C). Anything above 102°F (38.9°C) is abnormal. Taking the temperature is easy, but reading the thermometer may not be. So practise with your own stable thermometer whilst your horse is still healthy.

Heart and pulse rates are the same numerically; they are merely counted at different places. Counting the heart rate really needs a stethoscope to actually listen to the heart. The pulse rate is counted by resting a finger over the artery which passes over the bottom edge of the lower jaw and about half way along, and counting the faint pulsations. This can be difficult to do, and practice really is necessary. In a healthy horse at rest, the heart rate is around 40 per minute. If it is 60 or more per minute in a resting horse, there is something wrong. In a galloping horse the heart rate may exceed 200 per minute. Again in the resting horse, the respiratory rate (as measured by watching the horse's flanks and counting the number of breaths per minute) is much slower than after exercise. It will be around 8-16 breaths per minute. This relationship of three heart beats to each breath is maintained until the horse is undertaking really fast exercise. So if a horse seems to be breathing quickly, first of all check whether it is doing so

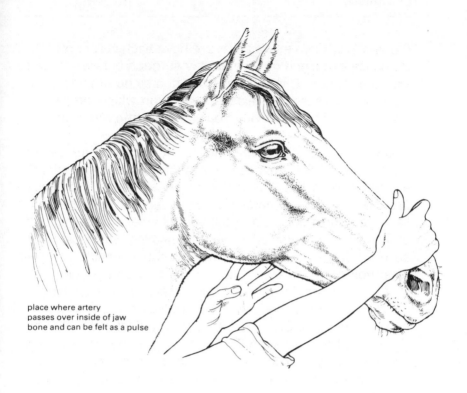

place where artery
passes over inside of jaw
bone and can be felt as a pulse

in relation to its heart rate.

The final two signs of health – temperament and feeding – are purely a subjective assessment based on careful observation. A veterinary surgeon will never be able to assess these factors, because he will not have had the opportunity to observe the horse for weeks and months. He will have to come to you, the owner, for this information. This does not make it any less valuable or scientific. The fact that a horse did not eat up a feed which it normally eats straightaway is often the very first sign of a problem, and enables us to look backwards to the very start of the disease.

In addition to knowing the general signs of health, it is important to know the veterinary status of each particular horse which you look after. You need to be aware of past scars, bony swellings and so on if you are to be able to distinguish new developments from existing problems. Perhaps

13

the best way to do this is always to have each new horse you purchase examined by a veterinary surgeon before you part with the money. This will avoid the heartache of finding out later that there is a pre-existing condition which affects the horse, and will also provide you with a written report on any defects.

During the chapters which follow, there are a number of occasions where I use the phrase 'seek immediate veterinary advice'. I mean just that. All veterinary surgeons in practice provide a 24-hour emergency telephone service. They will listen to your problem, and tell you whether it is something they need to see immediately or something which can wait several hours. If you are not knowledgeable enough to know what treatment you should be giving a problem, you are certainly not knowledgeable enough to take upon yourself the decision as to whether the veterinary surgeon should come now or tomorrow. Give your vet a ring, and let him make the decision. His name and telephone number should be engraved on your mind. It should also be prominently displayed in the tack room in case you are not around when an emergency arises.

Pasture Management

Horse owners must take active steps to improve the grass which their horse will be grazing during the spring and summer. All too often we expect Mother Nature to look after the grass while we devote all our efforts to improving our riding abilities or our horse's performance.

The first step to pasture improvement is regular topping of any areas of long grass. As you will have noticed, paddocks grazed exclusively by horses for any length of time become divided into 'lawns', where the grass is kept closely cropped by grazing, and 'rough', where the horses defaecate but do not graze. Topping limits the percentage of the paddock which turns into "rough' and so increases the area available for grazing. In any case, horses do not eat long grass nearly as readily as short grass.

Horse droppings should be picked up off the pasture on a regular basis to reduce the transmission of worms from one horse to another, or even from one horse back to itself. Of course, it is not much fun for us to be out collecting this during the bitter cold weather or the rain, but paddocks which are grazed during the winter can become heavily contaminated with faeces. If this is not removed before the spring, it will be impossible to find among the grass. Another encouragement to clean up the paddocks even during the winter time is that some worm eggs can survive for quite some time in faeces during winter, only to hatch all together when the warmer weather comes.

There are no chemicals which will kill worm eggs on pasture but, as will be discussed later, grazing with cattle and sheep can remove many of the horse worms.

Any farmer growing a crop commercially would take care to ensure that he used fertiliser and weedkillers at the right times to ensure a maximum harvest. Horse owners rarely use these aids, and I suspect it is because they cannot be bothered to learn how to use them safely.

Fertilisers can be very useful to stimulate grass growth in the spring. Without them it can take an unnecessarily long time for the grass to recover from the 'damaging' effect of being grazed during the winter. The harder the grass has been grazed, the more beneficial fertilisers can be.

Fertilisers are safe for use with horses, **as long as the paddock is not grazed until a good shower of rain has washed them into the ground** (which is not usually a very long wait in our climate). The grass that grows needs some care in its use, however. Fertilisers can only stimulate the production of lush young grass, they cannot make more old fibrous stems. So your horse will be having a change of diet, and needs to be treated accordingly.

The changeover to a fertilised paddock must be as gradual as the changeover from any food to another. The bacteria in the horse's large colon which digest the cellulose in grass have to change from a mixture which is best at handling tough old fibre to a mixture which can handle the high water content of new grass.

You must also remember that lush young grass tastes nicer than last year's old stuff. Left to itself, the horse may 'make a pig of itself'. So grazing may need to be temporarily restricted, either by reducing the available area or by stabling.

Weedkillers are potentially toxic chemicals. Many of them act either on the surface of the plant or by being taken in by the plant tissues. So unlike fertiliser, which is washed into the soil, a considerable amount of weedkiller may be present in plants above the ground. It is obvious that the manufacturer's instructions must be followed **exactly** with regard to the dilution rates, application rates and the period which needs to elapse before the paddock is grazed.

One problem is that many manufacturers fail to mention horses in their instructions, only stating when cattle and sheep can return to the field. There are weedkillers available that do consider the horse, so it is worth looking out for one of these. A general point is that a longer time should be allowed to elapse before grazing after weedkiller application in dry weather, when growth will be slower and less chemical washed off the plant, than in wet weather.

Ragwort is a particular problem because it is just as poisonous dead as it is alive, so if your weedkiller kills any ragwort the dead plants should be removed before grazing – it is surprising how willing horses can be to eat dead ragwort. In any case, the more 'weeds' that are killed off, the longer it might be wise to wait before grazing because of chemical residues in the dead plants. At certain times of year it may be necessary to reduce access to paddocks because of danger from trees present in or around the pasture. Oak trees pose a real threat as the acorns fall, because these are poisonous if eaten by horses. You will either need to remove the acorns or to remove the horses until the acorns have rotted away.

With proper pasture care, there is no reason why we should see any horses standing in sick pastures where the weeds are at least a foot tall but the grass never gets over half an inch high.

1 The First Aid Kit

The underlying principle of all first aid kits must be that they are for first aid. So they must be available at the time of the accident, or very soon after. It follows that there is no point in having only one first aid kit, and keeping that in the stable yard. When you go out for a long hack, you could find yourself miles from home with a wound which needs attention before you continue. Alternatively you might find yourself at an equestrian event of some kind, and have to go around neighbouring horseboxes trying to borrow first aid items which you really should have had available yourself. Ideally, therefore, you should have three first aid kits. The main kit should be kept in the stable yard. There should be another kit permanently in the horsebox or trailer, and a very small kit which you routinely put in a pocket or fasten to your belt whenever going off on a hack (in the same way that one always puts on a hard hat when going out on a ride).

The other point about a first aid kit is that it is only for the first aid. The aim is not to be able to treat major illnesses, or deal with major wounds, without seeking professional help. The aim of a first aid kit is not to make you completely independent of your vet, but to enable you to present the problem to him in a state that will enable him to achieve the best possible results.

In this chapter I shall discuss the various components which might be included in a first aid kit, to help guide your choice as to which to choose for your own situation.

DISINFECTANT

A disinfectant is not nearly as important as many people think. It is more important that wounds are clean and free from visible dirt than that they have been disinfected. Perhaps the most important role of the disinfectant in a first aid kit is to ensure that the water you use for cleaning a wound does not carry further infection which might cause additional contamination of the wound. After all, stable yard water supplies are often carried by plumbing which is not up to household standards. Equally, out in the field it may be possible to obtain water from a pond or stream, but that water also may be contaminated. Water sterilising tablets may therefore be just as useful in a first aid kit as a bottle of disinfectant. They will certainly take up less space, and weigh less.

When manufacturers prepare a disinfectant, they have to strike a balance between making it strong enough to kill bacteria and possible viruses, and yet not so irritant that it also kills off the body tissues with which is comes into contact. Indeed, this is one of the major differences between using a disinfectant on a wound and using an antibiotic. Antibiotics act directly on the bacteria and kill them without affecting the surrounding tissues at all, whereas disinfectants kill all living tissues. As long as you follow the manufacturer's instructions as to the dilution of the disinfectant, then you do not need to worry. You must at all costs avoid the temptation, though, to use the disinfectant at a stronger concentration than is recommended merely because the wound is particularly dirty. A stronger solution will not kill any more bacteria, but it may irritate the horse's tissues enough to slow down healing.

Whichever disinfectant you use, always make sure that you have an appropriate measure which will enable you to mix the solution up correctly. You should also be aware that many disinfectants are inactivated by organic matter. As a result, a dirty bucket of disinfectant may have no effect at all. It is better to change the water you are using and have to use plain water than it is to feel forced to carry on washing a wound with disinfectant solution which is getting dirtier and dirtier.

SKIN SWABS

Many horse owners will have noticed that veterinary surgeons often use small swabs impregnated with an antiseptic when they are either cleaning the skin before injecting a horse, or cleaning around the wound. These swabs are either packed in small paper envelopes, or are rolled inside a special container which prevents the antiseptic evaporating. The main advantage of these skin preparation swabs is that they make you completely independent of the water supply.

CLEANSING AGENTS

In recent years the use of cleansing agents has spread from the human to the veterinary field. These are basically a mixture of malic, benzoic and salycylic acids, and they act by aiding the loosening and removal of dead tissue from the wound. They also have antibacterial properties, which is an added bonus. Both cream and liquid formulations are available, and they make a very effective, and inexpensive, way of treating uncontaminated wounds.

WOUND POWDERS AND OINTMENTS

After a wound has been cleaned, it is customary to apply some form of ointment or powder in order to prevent new infections getting into the wound. You should be aware of the advantages and disadvantages of the various forms in which the drugs can be applied. Ointments are by their very nature oil-based. They need comparatively more effort to spread than creams, and are not as readily absorbed. On the other hand, they are water-resistant up to a point, and so not as readily washed away by rain or wet grass. Oily preparations of any kind, be they the 'green oils' which have caused such havoc to horse's wounds over the years, or oil-based ointments, should never be used on a wound which is going to be seen at a later stage by a vet. This is because if he then decides to stitch the wound, then all the oily dressing will need to be removed, and this can be rather difficult.

Wound creams are made with what is called a water-miscible base. This means that they are quite easy to rub into the skin, but that water from rain or from tissue fluid oozing out of the wound will wash the active substance away.

Wound powders have a great advantage over ointments and creams in that they can be applied without actually touching the horse. As wounds are usually painful to some extent, touching them to apply a drug may hurt the horse even more. Some horses will not let even their owners apply ointments or creams to a wound, but do not resent a puff of powder. The disadvantage of powders is the fact that they are dry. This means that the active ingredients are not absorbed through the skin at all. Only the area of the wound where the skin has been broken will have any contact with the drug. So a thick layer of powder does no more good than a very thin layer. It merely gives the horse owner a false feeling of security. It is far better to apply a very thin layer of powder several times a day than to apply a thick layer only once a day. A thick layer of powder also causes other problems in that moisture from a wound can be absorbed by the powder to form a kind of paste. The outside of this layer may look dry, but the layer next to the wound is wet and pussy. To ensure that this does not happen, it is advisable to remove the powder completely every 2-3 days, and start all over again with more thin dustings.

Aerosols can also be used to apply drugs to wounds without the need to touch the wound itself. Unfortunately they make a very distinctive noise, and horses can come to resent this. I think that the problem arises because aerosol sprays are cold when they evaporate on the skin, and the horse comes to associate the funny noise with the sudden cold around a painful area. Putting cotton wool into the horse's ears before spraying with an aerosol can make all the difference to the horse's behaviour. Once again the manufacturer's instructions should be noted. They usually state that the aerosol should be sprayed from a distance of 12-18in, not the 2-3in which so many people use. It is true that this greater distance results in a much larger area of the skin being sprayed, but it does give the correct concentration of application. The instructions also remind you to shake the can well before use. If you do not do so, the first half of the aerosol will be of a weaker concentration than it should be, and the second half will be much thicker than it should be. Aerosols do have a tendency for the nozzle to become blocked by dried spray, so it is worth cleaning the nozzle after you have used the spray.

So far I have not discussed which drugs may be useful for application to skin wounds. The first choice is between an antiseptic and an antibiotic. Antiseptic preparations are more readily available because they can be sold anywhere. Antibiotics, on the other hand, can only be obtained from veterinary surgeries. In my opinion antibiotics are far more effective at killing the bacteria which can infect wounds, and they do not damage the wound tissues at all. So it is worth calling in at your vet's surgery and asking for an antibiotic cream/powder/ spray. There are several antibiotics which are particularly useful in this situation. Neomycin is very widely used in creams, and tetracycline is the active ingredient of the 'blue spray' which many people obtain from their vet. I must point out that it is the antibiotic which is the active ingredient, not the blue colouring with which it is traditionally combined. There have even been manufacturers who have made aerosols which are readily available over the counter but whose only good point is that they colour the wound! Wound powders are often based on sulphonamide drugs, because these are very stable and can withstand more variation in temperature etc. than many other antibiotics. Incidentally, all antibiotic preparations now have an expiry date, and so you should routinely check your first aid kits to make sure that any expiry dates have not been exceeded.

FLY REPELLENTS

Most people will not think of fly repellents as being part of a first aid kit, but I have included them for two reasons. Firstly, because if a horse suffers from sweet-itch, you really need to be able to apply a fly repellent as soon as the horse starts rubbing itself rather than when you remember to buy the drug. Secondly, flies are always attracted to an open wound. When they land on the wound they cause irritation, and may cause the horse to rub the wound. They may also lay their eggs on the wound, so that it becomes fly-blown. It is possible to obtain wound powders which already contain a fly repellent, and it is obviously an especially good idea to use such powders during the summer months.

WOUND DRESSINGS

For a variety of reasons, it may be necessary to cover a wound. It is important when you do so to use a dressing which will not stick to the wound. If, for instance, you bandage straight over a wound, when you come to remove the bandage you will have to pull away the clot which has soaked into the bandage, and this is painful. Often the wound will also then start bleeding again, which is a nuisance.

One of the most popular non-stick dressings consists of gauze impregnated with an antibiotic ointment. This kills two birds with one stone, in that it prevents the bandage from sticking and also releases antibiotic to help control any infection. The tulle is packed in individual squares, so it takes up very little room in the first aid kit and is very light.

Another useful dressing is Mellolin. This consists of a special polythene membrane which will not stick to the wound, but which will allow fluid to pass through it. The membrane is backed onto a piece of lint, and this absorbs any fluid which passes through. A word of warning: some people feel tempted to apply Mellolin with the lint side towards the wound, which is completely wrong. Mellolin does not do anything to control infection, this has to be done in other ways, but it is very effective in keeping wounds slightly moist but not wet, in other words providing ideal conditions for skin to grow.

Granuflex is another dressing which concentrates on providing the sort of environment where wound healing can take place as rapidly as possible. It consists of a relatively thick layer of granules embedded in a type of jelly. The dressing is moulded to the shape of the wound and held in place for several days without changing. Seepage from the wound is absorbed by the jelly, which becomes rather gooey as a result. So wounds where Granuflex has been used look rather messy initially, but when they have been cleaned up they look surprisingly clean and dry.

COTTON WOOL

Most people have cotton wool in their first aid kit for the wrong reasons. It does not make a good means of absorbing water for cleaning wounds, because it tends to fall apart in the water. It does not make a good padding underneath bandages because it sticks to any moisture and leaves fluff behind when you remove it. In any case applying and removing cotton wool can be frustrating because it tears so readily.

Nevertheless, any major first aid kit must always include at least two unopened 500g packs of cotton wool, and preferably three. This is because it is a vital component of the Robert Jones splint which is used to immobilise any leg where there is even the slightest chance of a broken bone. The rolls are wrapped around the injured leg as tightly as is possible with cotton wool, and the whole dressing held in place by a very firm bandage. The sheer bulk of the cotton wool, and the way it compresses around the leg, immobilises the limb. As a result, if there is a fracture it will not be made many times worse by further movement of the bones. The temptation to open the packs of cotton wool and remove small amounts for various purposes must therefore be resisted at all costs. Otherwise when you really do need it, you will not have enough there to immobilise the limb properly.

GAMGEE TISSUE

Gamgee overcomes almost all the disadvantages of cotton wool from the first aid point of view. It consists of cotton wool held firmly between two layers of gauze. As a result it can be unrolled and applied very readily. It can be cut to shape, and will hold that shape. It does not leave fluff on the skin, wound or the first aider's hands. The major disadvantage is that it does not mould as well around joints or tapering legs as does cotton wool on its own. You should be aware that there are two 'qualities' of gamgee tissue — pink label and blue label. The latter is more expensive than the pink label, and so is sometimes sold to unsuspecting horse owners who really only need the pink label tissue.

BANDAGES

Probably the cheapest form of bandage is the WOW or white open weave bandage. These have no practical value for horses and, although sometimes included in specially purchased first aid boxes, should be discarded. They do not stretch to enable them to mould to the shape of the horse's leg, and they have no give at the edges, so that they really dig into the skin if put on tightly. Yet they always need to be put on tightly because the successive layers of bandage do not hold against each other, and so a WOW bandage rapidly slips and comes off.

The most suitable general purpose bandage for first aid use in horses is the crepe bandage. Its manufacture allows a degree of give both sideways, allowing it to adapt well to awkward shapes, and lengthways so that it can be applied firmly but still have room for further stretching if necessary. Traditionally the end of a crepe bandage is held in place by a safety pin. Some owners look askance at this, worrying what damage the pin will do if it comes undone. In my experience this is simply not a problem, and in any case crepe bandages are rarely left uncovered. At the very least there will be an ordinary stable bandage over them. Crepe bandages can be washed and used again, but they always lose some of their elasticity when this is done.

Self-adhering bandages do just what their name implies. Successive layers of the bandage stick to each other, but the bandage does not stick to skin or anything else. One advantage of this is that, once you have put the first layer of bandage in place, even if the horse kicks out and jerks the bandage out of your hand, what you have applied will not come undone and the unused roll will not unroll all across the stable. Self-adhering bandages will stretch during application, so that you can control how tight the bandage is as you put it on. The layers of bandage then stick to each other, however, so there is no further give in the bandage. If the leg swells up underneath the bandage, it is just as if the bandage was put on tighter. In most cases, therefore, inexperienced users should always bandage over a layer of gamgee tissue, in order to provide some elasticity should the leg swell. If you apply a self-adhering bandage to a leg which is originally swollen, but then the swelling goes down at all, the lack of elasticity again means that the bandage will not shrink and so the bandage will become loose. Self-adhering bandages are best used for support, rather than merely holding a dressing in place. They are much more expensive than crepe bandages, but look very smart because they conform so exactly to the shape of the leg, and do not need any visible means of securing the end of the bandage. They can be reused, but need very careful removal if they are not to be torn during the process. They can also be washed, but again care is needed so that they do not become hopelessly stuck to themselves during the process.

Elastic adhesive bandages are usually used only as the outer layer of a dressing. They are water-resistant and very tough. They stick quite well to hair, and so can anchor a dressing in place. Unfortunately when you come to remove them you are likely to pull the hairs of the horse's skin, and the horse may resent this. The adhesive is not always effective at low temperatures, so it may pay to warm the bandage slightly before use. This applies especially to the end of the bandage, which may come undone. Rubbing the end gently with your hand after you have applied it may help to persuade the adhesive to stick.

Stretch tubular net is sometimes used to hold initial dressings in place. It does not provide a firm enough hold to stop a dressing slipping on its own, or to provide any sort of worthwhile support to an injured leg.

Bandaging the joint of the horse's leg can be very difficult because of the shape and the amount of movement. The problem is that almost invariably the leg below the dressing is narrower than the leg inside the dressing. So the tighter you make the dressing, the more likely it is to slip downwards unless you have anchored it firmly. Pressage dressings provide a specialist, if expensive, answer to this problem. They are made of Lycra, and are the shape and size of each particular joint. They fasten down the side with first a velcro fastening and then a zip fastener.

POULTICES

The scientific value of poultices is doubtful. The theory is that they retain heat, and this increases the local blood supply to the area. Substances such as kaolin may also exert a drawing action pulling fluids including pus out of a wound, but this activity is only exerted over the very small area of the wound, it does not penetrate the skin. Kaolin can be used hot or cold, a point which is often forgotten. It heats up most quickly in small quantities, and this is made use of in the so-called instant poultices. These consist of a thin polythene envelope full of kaolin which is rapidly heated by immersion in hot water. Placing aluminium foil around the outside of a kaolin poultice helps it to retain its heat. The main disadvantage of kaolin is that, except in the envelope pack I have mentioned, it is difficult and messy to apply and remove. Yet if you do not remove the old kaolin from the wound before applying a new poultice, you will be losing all the 'drawing' effect.

Animalintex is a form of gamgee tissue which is impregnated with chemicals which give it the 'drawing' properties. The poultice has to be activated by soaking in warm water. It cannot be used to provide a cold compress. Animalintex is very convenient to use because you merely have to wrap it around the site where it is needed. Care is needed to ensure that the active side of the dressing is against the wound. When the poultice is removed, it leaves behind a gelatinous mass which has to be wiped away.

COLD PACKS

Cold can be applied in a variety of ways. Bandages can be soaked in cold water. Ice can be wrapped between the layers of bandage. Even a pack of frozen peas can, in an emergency, be wrapped around a horse's leg. There are flexible packs available which are similar to those used to keep food cool on picnics. These are cooled in a deep freeze, and hold their low temperature for a relatively long time, although even after a couple of hours it is amazing how warm the surface is next to the horse's skin. The Bonner bandage is a specially designed bandage which absorbs moisture and is still flexible enough to be applied to the leg even when that water is still frozen. Because it is so closely applied all around the area, it has a very effective cooling action.

SCISSORS

Every first aid kit must contain a good pair of sharp scissors. They should have rounded ends to the blades so that there is no danger of a sudden movement jabbing a blade into the horse.

THERMOMETER

A thermometer is also needed in the stable first aid kit. The horse's temperature is taken by holding the thermometer in the horse's rectum for approximately one minute. Unless you use one of the new electronic thermometers which give a digital read-out, it takes practice to read a clinical thermometer. Make sure that you are not having to practise when you really need to know the result accurately because you have a sick horse. **The normal temperature of a healthy horse is around 101-101.5°F or 38.5°C.**

FIRST AID KIT REQUIREMENTS

First Aid Item		Stable Kit	Travelling Kit	Pocket Kit
Disinfectant		Yes	Possibly	No
Skin Swabs		Yes	Yes	Yes
Cleansing Agent		Yes	Possibly	No
Wound powder/ointment/aerosol		Yes	Yes	No
Fly Repellent		Yes	No	No
Wound Dressing:	tulle	Yes	Yes	Yes
	Mellolin	Yes	No	No
	Granuflex	Possibly	No	No
Cotton Wool		Two	Two	No
Gamgee Tissue		Yes	Yes	No
Bandages:	crepe	Two	Yes	Possibly
	self-adherent	Yes	Yes	Possibly
	elastic adhesive	Yes	No	No
	tubular net	Possibly	No	No
Poultice:	kaolin	Choose one	No	No
	Animalintex		No	No
Cold Pack:	Tendoneze	Choose one	Choose one	No
	Bonner bandage			No
Scissors		Yes	Yes	No
Thermometer		Yes	No	No

MAKING A CHOICE

The stable first aid kit should ideally contain at least one item from each of the above categories. In the bandage category there should be at least two crepe bandages plus either a self-adhering bandage or an elastic adhesive bandage. The horsebox kit can omit fly repellent, the thermometer and the poultices (which would need heating up anyway). Wherever possible it should include some means of applying cold to an injured part of the body. In most cases this will mean remembering before leaving for the event to prepare a cold box in which to transport your chosen item. The hacking kit may consist simply of a skin preparation swab, a non-stick wound dressing and a crepe or self-adherent bandage. The total weight of such a kit is only about 45g, and it takes up very little more space than a bandage. Yet it provides a basis for treating many minor problems.

During the following chapters I shall deal with the major practical problems which affect each part of the horse's body. In discussing any appropriate first aid, I shall assume that a full first aid kit is available.

2 The Skin

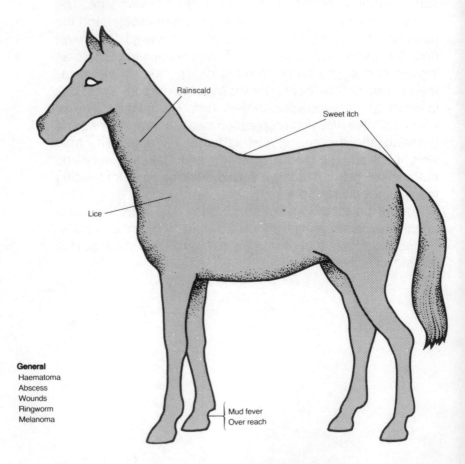

Rainscald

Sweet itch

Lice

General
Haematoma
Abscess
Wounds
Ringworm
Melanoma

Mud fever
Over reach

The skin is the horse's main defence against infection. Whenever the skin is breached, it is possible for bacteria from the environment to gain entry into the body as a whole. The skin is waterproof, but that does not prevent it from being softened by constant exposure to moisture, in the same way that the skin of our hands becomes softened after washing dishes. Mud fever is an example of an infection which relies on the skin becoming softened to allow the infection to establish itself.

The skin consists of not one but many layers of cells. The bottom layers are living cells which are multiplying in number. The top layers are dead cells. If bacteria or parasites can penetrate down beneath the superficial layers, they will be protected not only from the environment but also from many forms of medication we might use to kill them. For this reason treatment for skin conditions must be continued for quite some time, and certainly for longer than it takes for the surface symptoms to disappear.

The horse sweats from its skin. The whole surface has some sweat glands, but there is a higher concentration in areas such as the neck, shoulders and flanks. The main reason for sweating is to cool the body. During exercise more energy is released in the form of heat than is ever released for muscle movement. This heat has to be removed if it is not to cause damage to the internal structures. The evaporation of sweat off the skin surface absorbs heat, and so cools the body. It is important to realise that merely producing sweat does not cool the horse. So a horse which is literally dripping with sweat is not necessarily being cooled at all. Only if the atmospheric conditions allow the sweat to evaporate will there be any cooling effect.

Man has taken it upon himself to interfere with the horse's skin structure, to the extent that we remove much of the hair by clipping during the winter. It is worth remembering that a clipped horse loses more heat by radiation from its body than an unclipped horse, and so will require more energy from its food unless it is well rugged up. A clipped horse loses its sweat more quickly by running off the smooth surface, and so sweating works less efficiently. A clipped horse may suffer more minor abrasions in areas deprived of the protection from hair. Finally, a clipped horse may well suffer many minute knicks in its skin during the act of clipping. If you do not observe scrupulous hygiene with the clipping equipment, then these wounds may easily become infected.

ABSCESSES

An abscess is an accumulation of pus. Skin abscesses actually have the pus underneath the skin, rather than within the skin layer itself. There are certain basic features of an abscess which enable us to differentiate it from other skin swellings. To a large extent these are the classic signs of inflammation.

So an abscess causes a swelling due to the accumulation of the pus. If the abscess lies over a soft part of the body, such as a muscle, then the swelling may not appear so noticeable as it does if the abscess lies over a hard area such as a bone, where all of the swelling is forced outwards.

An abscess is warm to the touch. This is because the blood supply to an inflamed area is drastically increased, and the warmth we feel over an abscess is simply warmth from the increased blood supply to the affected skin.

An abscess is painful. This is partly due to the release of certain chemicals as the horse's body fights the infection. It is also due to the abscess occupying a space under the skin where there wasn't a space before. The abscess literally dissolves a space for itself and pushes the other tissues apart.

By definition, an abscess contains fluid which we call pus. This consists partly of tissue fluid, partly of dead and dying white blood cells (especially the cells called neutrophils), and partly of live and dead bacteria. An abscess either starts because a bacterium circulating in the blood stream becomes lodged in a particular area and multiplies there, or the skin layer is broken and the bacterium gains entry through a wound. As the bacteria start to multiply, they attract neutrophils to the area and the resulting inflammatory reaction results in the release of the fluid. I mentioned earlier that pus can eat a space for itself. It also tends to eat a hole through which the pus can drain out onto the surface of the skin. So initially an abscess feels quite hard. Then it softens as the pus accumulates. Then one area of the overlying skin starts to thin, and eventually the pus bursts out at this point. The pus does not always burst out at the lowest point of the abscess, and so even a burst abscess will not always completely drain of pus.

Action

Pus is always better out than in, so **we must encourage any attempt by an abscess to open to the surface. Warm fomentations** (not hot or you will scald the skin) **can easily be applied** by holding or, if possible, bandaging cloths soaked in warm water over the whole area. It is surprising how much relief from pain this can give the horse, even when you can only hold the fomentation in place for 10-15 minutes at a time. A vet may decide to lance the abscess with a scalpel in order to release the pus at an advantageous place for drainage.

Once the abscess is draining, **poulticing may help to draw out the pus**. You should be aware that poulticing the skin for too long may lead to the skin edges dying and so prolong eventual healing.

Antibiotics will obviously help the horse's own defences to kill the bacteria. The use of sprays and creams around the abscess is of very little value. It is the deeper parts of the abscess where the antibiotics are needed, the parts from which the pus cannot drain so well. In addition to injectable antibiotics, there are now a range of preparations for horses which are based on the trimethoprim mixture of antibiotics. These can be given by mouth in powder or paste form.

Pus contains living bacteria as well as dead ones. So pus from one abscess can infect other wounds. **Wash the skin around an abscess regularly to keep it clean. If large amounts of pus are discharging, cover the area below the abscess with Vaseline** to protect the skin surface from scalding by the pus.

Any tack which has been in contact with the pus must be disinfected, as should any contaminated parts of the stable.

HAEMATOMAS

Because haematomas also cause swelling underneath the skin, they can easily be confused with abscesses. Haematomas do not, however, show the classic signs of inflammation. So they are not warm to the touch, and they are not painful. The swelling is caused by the release of blood from a ruptured blood vessel under the skin. This blood does not clot readily, and so if some of the fluid is drawn off through a needle, it looks like fresh blood. In time the blood cells sediment out from the serum, and a sample at that time will produce straw-coloured fluid with red tinges.

Action
No action is required. If the blood is drained out of a haematoma during the first couple of weeks after it has formed, then it will only reform within hours. In time the body will remove the fluid and blood cells, leaving only a small amount of fibrous tissue. Very occasionally surgical drainage is carried out.

Watch that the haematoma does not become secondarily infected with bacteria from the blood stream, causing an abscess to form.

How to tell the difference between an Abscess and an Haematoma		
Symptom	Abscess	Haematoma
Swelling	Yes	Yes
Fluid filled	Yes	Yes
Pain	Yes	No
Heat	Yes	No
Action: needs lancing	**Yes**	**No**

LICE

Lice are small parasites which live on and in the skin. They are visible to the naked eye, but we often fail to see them because of the horse's thick coat and the fact that their dark colour blends into the dark skin and coat of the horse. What we do see are the areas where the horse has rubbed itself bald in response to the irritation caused by the biting or blood-sucking activities of the lice. If the condition is not controlled, the horse may rub large raw patches on its skin. The neck is the commonest area to be affected.

Lice live on horses all the year round. It is only usually in the cold winter months, however, that we see the signs of their presence. This is because the thicker winter coat protects them, and they are more active during cold weather anyway. Lice are contagious, so if horses are turned out in a field or yard together the parasites will spread from one horse to another.

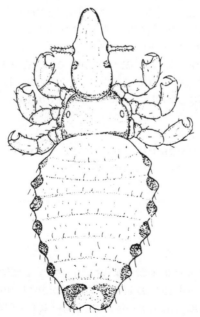

Fig 1 The sucking louse (Haematopinus asini) (from The Horse's Health from A to Z)

Action
The horse should be thoroughly washed in a shampoo containing piperonyl butoxide and pyrethrum. Make sure that you follow the manufacturer's instructions precisely. The anthelmintic drug, ivermectin, also kills lice, although it may need several doses of the oral preparation to kill off new parasites as they hatch out on the horse.

Tack used on the affected horse should also be washed with the same shampoo as is used on the horse, but the parasite cannot live off the horse for any appreciable length of time and so stables and other accommodation cannot become a risk to other horses.

MELANOMA

A melanoma is a tumour which originates from the black pigment cells, usually in the skin. The tumour has a rounded, knobbly appearance. It is hard but painless to the touch. They are especially common in grey horses, although they can occur in all colours of horse. It has been suggested that 80 per cent of greys have at least one melanoma. The commonest place for them to occur is underneath the tail.

Action
No action is necessary. The tumours are not usually malignant, and do not affect the horse.

MUD FEVER

Mud fever is a skin infection which usually affects the skin of the lower legs, but can extend right up the legs or affect parts of the lower body. It causes the development of raw areas which ooze a mixture of pus and serum. This then hardens into a scab. When the skin at the back of the pastern region is affected, around the heels, cracks may develop in the skin which gives rise to the mistaken impression that the original problem was an over-reach (see Fig 4, p83).

Mud fever is more common on skin with white hairs rather than pigmented hairs. This is thought to be due to a lack of resistance to infection in such unpigmented skin. The infection can also establish itself more readily in skin which has been softened by frequent contact with water, and so readily occurs in the muddy conditions which have contributed to its name. Mud also abrades the skin, causing small grazes where the infection can establish itself. However, dry dusty conditions will also cause such abrasions, and so the infection is also found in these conditions, especially in Australia where it is known as Queensland itch.

The bacterium which causes the problem is called *Dermatophilus congolensis*. It is a very successful bacterium because once it has become established on a horse, it can survive for many months. In this respect it is helped by the crusts which form a protective umbrella over the living bacteria, and protect them from drying out.

Action

In the laboratory *Dermatophilus* is very readily killed off by almost any antiseptic or antibiotic. Mud fever on the horse, however, can be resistant to every ointment rubbed into it. The reason for this discrepancy is the protective effect of the scabs, held in place by the horse's hair.

The first stage of treatment is to **clip away all the hairs on the affected area.** If necessary, the horse must be sedated to enable you to do so.

Next **the area must be kept free from any scabs.** This is best achieved by **washing the area in a good antiseptic shampoo every third day,** and literally picking off all the scabs whilst the shampoo is in place. **The skin should then be thoroughly dried** in order to prevent further softening of the skin and moist conditions for bacterial growth. It is better to have raw areas of skin than scabs. If even one scab remains then there are thousands of protected bacteria left behind. **At**

least once a day between shampoos any scabs which have reformed should be removed. Initially many scabs will form, but as treatment gets the infection under control, the number of scabs you need to remove will be drastically reduced.

Finally **an antibiotic ointment should be applied to the affected area twice daily.**

Prevention consists of careful drying of susceptible areas whenever you return from exercise. It may help to apply a waterproof barrier over the skin of the heels and over any areas which have been affected in the past. This can be achieved by using a human barrier cream, an udder cream, or as a last resort Vaseline. I put the latter as a last resort because, although it provides a good waterproof barrier, it also provides a protective layer over any infection which manages to get underneath it, and the Vaseline is then difficult to remove.

OEDEMA

Strictly speaking oedema is not a skin condition, but it affects the skin and underlying tissues. Oedema is the swelling which is due to an accumulation of fluid in the small spaces in and under the skin. The swelling may be cold or warm to the touch, depending on its underlying cause. When it occurs on the body, it produces raised areas; when it occurs down the legs it just produces localised swelling. The fluid arises from a number of causes, which are mentioned under the individual ailments, but the basic cause is leakage of the fluid out of the veins which supply that particular area.

The swelling due to oedema can be differentiated from that due to other causes by the fact that it pits with pressure. In other words, if you press a finger into the swelling and then remove it, a depression remains where you removed your finger.

Action

The first aid treatment for oedema is the application of cold. This reduces the blood supply to the area, and so reduces the amount of leakage of tissue fluid from that blood supply. When oedema occurs down the legs, **bandaging may restrict further swelling.** It is important to extend the bandage above and below the swelling because otherwise the bandage will dig into the surrounding oedematous skin and cause further problems. Diuretics can be used to prevent or reduce oedema. These are drugs which increase the amount of urine which is formed. As a result the horse's body looks for extra supplies of fluid to replace that lost in the urine, and draws fluid from the oedema. The commonest effective diuretic is a drug called frusemide. Potassium nitrate is also sometimes used as a mild stable remedy.

OVER-REACH

An over-reach is a wound on the heels of the front legs which has been caused by the horse striking itself with one of its own hind legs. So it is impossible to get an over-reach on a hind leg. If there appears to be one, then mud fever is a more likely cause of the problem.

Because of the way in which it occurs, an over-reach always has a considerable amount of bruising around the wound, and it is also contaminated with dirt from the very moment that it is formed. The result is that over-reaches do not heal very well.

Action

Firstly the over-reach must be cleaned up. If it is severely contaminated with dirt, **an Animalintex poultice may be applied for a couple of hours.** Do not leave it on too long, however, as this will lead to softening and death of the skin edges of the wound. An antibiotic dressing should then be applied and **the wound covered with a protective dressing.** If in mild cases the horse is to continue being exercised without a bandage, then a barrier cream should be applied immediately before exercise, and the wound cleaned and dried immediately after exercise. Any swelling of the pastern should result in your seeking veterinary advice in order that antibiotic therapy can be started at once. Veterinary advice should also be sought over large fresh over-reaches which might need to be stitched.

How to tell the difference between an overreach and mud fever		
Symptom	Overreach	Mud Fever
Can affect front legs	Yes	Yes
Can affect hind legs	No	Yes
Sudden onset	Yes	No
Fresh bleeding wound at start	Yes	No
Swelling up pastern	Yes	Yes
Scab formed	Red blood in scab	Yellowish crusting scab

RAINSCALD

Rainscald is an infection of the upper surfaces of the horse's body which is caused by the same *Dermatophilus* bacterium that causes mud fever. In the case of rainscald the raw areas of the skin are very small, and the scabs which form hold together small groups of hairs. The impression is often of small paintbrush-like tufts of hair.

The infection comes from the environment whenever the ideal warm, humid conditions occur, and the affected areas often look as if they have been poured over the horse because they follow the paths that rain and sweat would as they run off the body. Rainscald is not caused by any overheating of the blood. Nor is it caused by too rich a diet.

Action

The horse should be given an antiseptic shampoo. A cheap alternative is washing in copper sulphate solution (1oz/25g in 1 gallon/4.5l of water). The scabs should be removed with a brush. Thorough drying is essential after the shampoo, and the whole process should be repeated after 3 days.

RINGWORM

Despite its name, this skin condition is nothing to do with a worm and does not necessarily bear any resemblance to a ring. It is a fungal infection of the skin and hair. Small hairless patches of rather crusty skin appear, which may or may not be round in shape. The patches are not inflamed, and do not appear to cause the horse any irritation. The hair loss is due to the weakened hairs breaking off rather than their being rubbed away.

Ringworm can occur anywhere on the horse's body, but is commonest in places which might be rubbed by tack. This is because the fungal spores need a small break in the skin in order to establish themselves initially. Ringworm is very contagious from one horse or its tack to another. Because it has a long incubation period (there is often a gap of 2-3 months between the spore landing on the skin and the appearance of the first skin patch) a horse may be infectious to other horses even before the owner is aware that the horse has the disease.

Action

An infected horse should be kept separate from other horses. It should be treated with an antibiotic skin wash (not a patent medicine ringworm dressing which will merely cover the fungus and not actually kill it). **All the tack** which might have been used on the horse during recent months **should be washed in either the same antibiotic** or in a strong disinfectant which is effective against ringworm. The stable, especially any rough surfaces such as wood, should be similarly treated. An antibiotic called **griseofulvin should be given orally for 7 days**. The drug must not be used in pregnant mares.

Do not believe old wives tales about ringworm being killed off by sunlight or being out to grass. It is true that ringworm will cure itself after about 3 months, so all sorts of 'treatments' will work after that period of time. Unfortunately during those months the fungus will have been passed on to many more horses.

It is always worth treating ringworm properly because it is a disease which can spread to human beings.

SWEET ITCH

Sweet itch is an irritation of the skin caused by a hypersensitivity to the bites of small midges. This irritation usually affects the area along the mane and at the base of the tail. It is so great that the horse will rub off all the mane and tail at affected areas, and the underlying skin may become raw and oozing with serum. With time the skin also becomes very thickened. The midges are only active during the summer months, and so the condition disappears during the winter. Once a horse has become hypersensitive in this way, it will always remain so and will suffer from sweet itch every succeeding summer.

Action
The horse must be protected from the bites of the midges. **As the insects are at their most active during the early hours of daylight and in the evening, the horse should not be left out in the field at this time.** Many people make the mistake of stabling affected horses during the heat of the day, and turning them out during the very time when the mites are biting most. The horse should only be turned out for 5-6 hours around midday. During the rest of the time it should be stabled, preferably with mosquito netting over any open doors and windows.

Fly repellants will help to keep the midges at bay, but they may well need to be applied every day,and not every week as is sometimes suggested in the products' advertising. Fly repellant strips and/or sprays should also be used in the stable.

Benzyl benzoate lotion helps to soothe the raw areas, and also helps to repel midges. Long lasting corticosteroid injections will reduce the horse's sensitivity and so the severity of the symptoms. Unfortunately they only last 10-14 days and carry a risk of causing laminitis.

WARTS

It is important to differentiate between the small warts which often appear around a horse's face, especially on young horses, and the much larger wart-like tumours which appear all over the body. These tumours are called sarcoids. They often occur on the skin down the inside of the legs, what might be called the 'legpit' area. They can become very large, and because of the places where they occur they often rub raw and then fail to heal. The raw, oozing mass may become infected, which makes it even more inflamed.

Action
The small warts need no action, although they may be present in very large numbers, and may appear to spread from one young horse to another. They will almost always disappear with time.

Sarcoids do not disappear, and tend to increase in size as well as number. **If the sarcoid has a distinct neck, then tying a fine thread tightly around it may cause most of the tumour to die and fall off. Small flat sarcoids may respond to human wart ointments.** Up to 50 per cent of sarcoids recur after surgical removal. Radiotheraphy, cryosurgery (freezing) and injecting with BCG vaccine appear to be more successful treatments.

45

WOUNDS

It is not possible in a book such as this to deal with every kind of wound which might occur. Anyone who has kept horses for any length of time will know that there are an amazing number of ways in which horses can cut themselves.

Action

An immediate decision should be made as to whether the wound needs stitching. By and large I would suggest that **any wound over one inch long should be stitched. Smaller wounds should be stitched if they are in such a position that they gape open.** Wounds on the body heal better than wounds on the legs, and the further down the legs you go, the less likely the wound is to heal perfectly by what we call first intention healing. Even if the stitches in a wound do not hold (and the period around the eighth day is the time when they will give way if they are going to do so) the sutures will have served to hold the deeper tissues together and to stop further infection gaining entry into the wound.

Clean wounds wherever possible, but do not expect bleeding to stop if you keep on washing the wound. Continued washing only washes the clots away as quickly as they are formed.

If the wound continues to bleed, firm pressure should be applied to it. This applies whether the wound is merely oozing slightly or whether blood is spurting out of it: only the amount of pressure which you will need to apply, and the size of the dressing, will alter. Wherever possible **use a non-stick dressing next to the wound** so that you will not dislodge the clot when you replace the dressing. **Wounds should be kept covered until they are dry to the touch and have stopped oozing,** so that they will not become secondarily infected when left exposed.

It should not be necessary to have an injection of tetanus antitoxin after a wound, because all horses should be fully protected by an up-to-date vaccination programme. **If you are unsure of the horse's vaccinal status, perhaps be-**

cause it is a very recent purchase, then tetanus antitoxin should be given.

The horse has a great tendency to form proud flesh during wound healing. This means that the wound fills with a pink fibrous tissue which continues to grow until it projects above the level of the surrounding skin. The surface layers of skin will not grow uphill, and so will not cover such a lump of proud flesh, which may remain as a permanent blemish. If such proud flesh appears to be forming, veterinary advice should be sought with a view to 'burning' it back with caustic preparations. Copper sulphate powder and cream are commonly used for this purpose, although in severe cases the proud flesh may need to be physically removed.

3 The Respiratory System

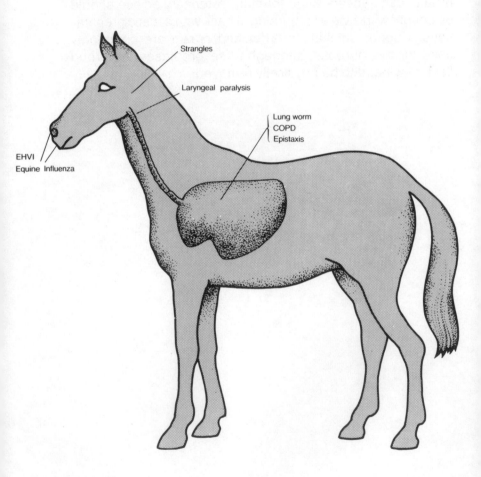

Strangles

Laryngeal paralysis

Lung worm
COPD
Epistaxis

EHVI
Equine Influenza

The process of life in every cell of a mammal such as the horse depends on the availability of oxygen. This oxygen is obtained from the air by sucking it into the lungs and allowing it to come into close contact with the blood stream (separated by only the thickness of one cell). The red blood cells take on board the oxygen, and give up carbon dioxide into the air, which is then pushed out of the body. You will appreciate that the air travels along quite a length of tubing before it reaches the lungs and the blood stream. Any factor which interferes with the air flow affects the amount of oxygen available to the blood. So the respiratory system is the first limiting factor for a horse's athletic performance. A horse can have the most efficient heart and circulatory system in the world, and receive the best quality food in the world, but if there is some factor decreasing the availability of oxygen, then its performance will be affected.

The horse's nostrils change in shape depending on the amount of air it requires. A galloping horse will have nostrils which are flared wide open. Flared nostrils in a horse which has not been galloping may indicate that there is some obstruction to the airflow lower down for which the body is trying to compensate. Air then passes over the turbinate bones in the head, which help to warm the air up before it goes on to the sensitive tissues of the lungs. The throat region is perhaps the most critical from the point of view of the upper airway. The air passes into a chamber called the pharynx at the back of the mouth. Here it has to enter the larynx through the vocal cords. But the position of the larynx is dependent on the soft palate, which supports it and should prevent food being able to get into the larynx instead of going down the oesophagus. In the resting horse, the vocal cords hang down like curtains across the larynx, almost but not quite closing the airway. With increasing exercise these 'curtains' open to allow more air to pass through.

The trachea is a long straight tube which stretches from the larynx right down the neck to the lungs. In the standing horse, this means that it runs down at an angle, which is unfortunate if any fluid has to be removed from the lungs. When the horse feeds with its head on the ground, such mucus can drain out by gravity. At other times, the horse relies on the activity of millions of tiny hairs, or cilia, which line the wall of the trachea and which move in a wave-like motion to lift the mucus up the trachea.

Just before the lungs, the airway starts to divide. First it divides into two bronchi, one leading to each lung, then the bronchi divide into smaller bronchioles, and finally the bronchioles lead into the alveoli, or air sacs, where the actual transfer of oxygen and carbon dioxide takes place. The system has to be kept moist, in order to counteract the drying effect of the passage of so much air. So mucus is secreted by cells lining the alveoli. In the normal horse the amount of mucus formed is so small that it never accumulates, and very little needs to be removed by the cilia. As a result a normal horse does not have much visible mucus in its trachea if we examine the horse's respiratory tract with a flexible endoscope, and nor does it have a discharge from its nostrils. If the lung tissue becomes inflamed for any reason, two main things happen: the amount of mucus formed is increased, and the alveolar walls become thickened.

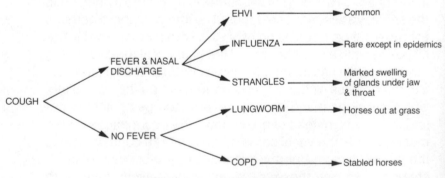

Fig 2 Diagnosing the coughing horse

CHRONIC OBSTRUCTIVE PULMONARY DISEASE (COPD)

Chronic obstructive pulmonary disease is the modern name for an old problem which used to be called heaves or broken wind. The name describes the cause of the horse's respiratory problem, namely the fact that the small airways down in the lungs are chronically obstructed. This obstruction is partly due to the fact that the airways, or bronchioles, are constricted by spasm of the muscles in their walls. This is called broncho-constriction. The obstruction is also caused by the accumulation of thick mucus which blocks the airways. This mucus is formed by the inflamed linings of the air sacs, or alveoli.

COPD is caused by a hypersensitivity reaction to fungal spores which are breathed in from hay and straw. So it is not merely any old dust which triggers off the condition, it is almost invariably the spores. This is important when it comes to considering prevention of the problem, because a horse bedded on sawdust is exposed to dust, but it is not at risk from COPD unless it is also exposed to fungi on hay. It should be appreciated that most of the dust particles which are big enough to be seen are too big to penetrate right down into the horse's lungs. They are filtered out higher up the respiratory tract. COPD is permanent, in that once a horse becomes hypersensitive, it will remain so. With careful management it may not show any symptoms for years and years, but as soon as its lungs are challenged again with spores, they will react and broncho-constriction will occur. The condition is also cumulative. The longer the period for which the horse is exposed to the fungi and the greater the number of spores to which it is exposed, the more alveoli become constricted. The symptoms thus gradually get worse and worse as the stabling period goes on.

The first symptom of COPD is often a nasal discharge, which may be most marked during feeding or first thing in the morning. Many owners fail to attach any importance to such a

constant symptom, considering it to be normal for that particular horse. As the number of constricted bronchioles
increases, the horse's athletic performance decreases. Again
this might not be very noticeable unless the horse is regularly
undertaking really strenuous work. The symptom which finally
sounds the alarm bells for most owners is the development of
a cough, especially when the horse or groom is moving
around in the stable and stirring up the bedding. The cough
reflects the horse's attempts to free some of the thick mucus
which is blocking the airways. As the condition progresses it
starts to really affect the way the horse breathes. The respiratory rate at rest increases from the 8-12 breaths per
minute seen in a normal horse to 20 breaths per minute or
more. The character of each breath also changes. Normally
breathing in is a muscular act and then expiration occurs by
the reflex relaxation of the muscles involved. In COPD the
force of this relaxation may not be sufficient to overcome the
resistance of the mucus-blocked airways. The horse then has
to add a muscular effort at the end of expiration in order to
empty the lungs. Expiration thus takes place in two separate
sections, hence the expression 'broken wind'. At the same
time the muscles responsible become better developed. We
can see the lower border of the muscles as a sloping groove
along the horse's abdomen. This is the so-called heave line.

Action
**Most horses return to normal if permanently turned out
to pasture.** If this is not possible, then the horse should be
stabled for as short a period as possible, and a strict clean-air
regime should be implemented. **The horse should never be
bedded on straw.** Wood shavings, shredded paper or peat
should be used. These must be kept clean and dry. If they are
allowed to become warm and damp, like a deep litter system,
then they too will become contaminated with fungi. **The
stable should be dust-free** to start with, and there should
not be any means by which the air space can communicate
with the air from adjacent straw-bedded stables. **Good venti-
lation should be in use all the time,** eg the top stable door

should never be closed. Care must also be taken that the stable is not down wind of danger sources such as the manure heap, hay or straw stack.

Clean Air Regime
1 Empty stable of all bedding
2 Hoover away all dust, including ceilings and walls
3 Make sure no air contact with adjoining stables
4 Make sure ventilation is open and working
5 Use wood shavings, peat or paper bedding
6 Keep bedding clean and dry

Ideally no hay should be fed, and this can be achieved by using proprietary complete horse nuts. Unfortunately these also reduce the time the horse can spend eating, and there can sometimes be problems associated with boredom. Vacuum-packed cut grass, such as Propack, is a good hay substitute, and indeed it has a better nutritional value than most good hays. Care must be taken in storage not to puncture the polythene bag around each bale. Once a bale has been opened it should be used up quickly because it very rapidly becomes contaminated with fungi from the atmosphere. Silage is another alternative to hay, but Big Bale Silage should be avoided because of the risk of contamination with botulism.

Many people place great reliance on soaking hay to reduce its danger. Unless you use continuously running water, the number of spores removed will be small. All that is achieved is that most of the spores become stuck to the wet strands of hay. This rapidly dries out around the outside of the hay net (which is the part which the horse can reach to eat) and so any effect will be short-lasting. Special machines are available which literally vacuum the hay clean of spores. The amount of hay fed can also be reduced by adding dried alfalfa products to the diet. Surprisingly few owners appear to be aware that **it is possible to test hay in order to assess the risk it presents from its fungal contamination.** This is carried out using a slit air sampler which deposits a sample of any dust present on the hay onto a special microscope slide.

Hay which has little or no contamination with spores is quite safe to buy.

There are drugs which can help in the treatment of COPD. Clenbuterol, given in the feed, has proved effective in relieving the broncho-constriction and returning the horse to apparent normality as long as it is coupled with a clean air regime. Sodium cromoglycate, which is administered via a nebuliser, can be used once the horse is symptom-free to prevent the release of histamine and other substances in the lungs which trigger off the whole process. This may allow limited exposure to hay and straw without causing any further problems.

EQUINE HERPES VIRUS TYPE I

Equine herpes virus type I (EHVI) is basically a respiratory virus, although it does also cause abortion in mares and can cause paralysis. It is a very common infection, and might be considered as the common cold of the horse. When the virus enters a yard we see a variety of reactions depending on the immunity of the individual horses. Some horses will show absolutely no symptoms at all, whereas others may be quite ill. It is a feature of EHVI that some horses may become latent carriers of the virus. They suffer repeated attacks without developing any immunity. After a natural infection with EHVI the immunity usually only last about 6 months.

The first symptom of EHVI infection is usually a rise in temperature. However, as this often occurs before the horse even appears ill, the owner may be unaware that the horse has had a fever. Indeed, it is often more rewarding to take the temperatures of in-contact horses rather than horses which are already obviously affected. The horse develops a nasal discharge which is clear at first, but which can become thick and pussy. The horse also starts to cough, and may continue to do so for a couple of weeks to a varying extent. The lymph nodes around the throat and under the jaw may be slightly swollen. Some horses remain surprisingly well through all of this, but most will be off-colour for at least a few days. In horses which are under stress, such as race horses in training, there may be a loss of performance which can persist for several months.

Diagnosis of EHVI is often made simply on the grounds that there is an infectious cough present. A precise diagnosis is now possible, however. A swab taken from the horse's nose may enable the virus to be cultured and rapidly identified. Unfortunately this is most successful when it is carried out during the temperature rise, which I have explained may not be detectable. Alternatively, a blood sample taken 10-14 days after the start of the infection can be compared with one taken when the symptoms first became noticeable in order to show which virus has stimulated a marked rise in immunity.

Action
Whenever there is a respiratory infection present, **it is always a good idea to institute a clean air regime (see page 53). There are no drugs which will kill the actual virus itself, but that does not mean that no treatment is necessary**. Recent research has shown that much of the exercise-induced pulmonary haemorrhage (see page 56) which occurs is due to the preventable after-effects of earlier respiratory virus infections. Antibiotics are only of value in treating any secondary infections which might become established in the lungs. Mucolytics, such as Sputolosin, help to reduce the viscosity of the mucus formed in the lungs, and thus make it easier for the horse to remove it. Clenbuterol also helps to prevent the accumulation of mucus by ensuring that the airways remain open. Incidentally, we should not seek to stop the coughing just for the sake of removing the most obvious symptom. The horse relies on coughing to get rid of much of the mucus from the lungs.

Although **isolation and hygiene measures such as disinfection of tack have a role in preventing the spread of EHVI,** they are often rather like shutting the stable door after the horse has bolted unless they are practised routinely with all horses which have been in contact with 'foreign' horses and so might introduce the infection into the yard. There are now effective vaccines available to protect against the respiratory symptoms of EHV1. As with natural infection, immunity is short lasting and 6-monthly boosters are required after initial vaccination.

EXERCISE-INDUCED PULMONARY HAEMORRHAGE

Exercise-induced pulmonary haemorrhage (EIPH) used to be called epistaxis. The change in name is significant. EIPH draws attention to the fact that the haemorrhage comes from the lungs, and that is triggered off by exercise. Epistaxis, on the other hand, merely means a nose bleed, and although the blood may appear at the nostrils it may not. In fact only about 10 per cent of the horses which have bleeding from the lungs after strenuous exercise actually have any blood appear at the nostrils, so the condition is far more widespread than ever appears to the eyes of horseowners. Only since the development of the fibreoptic endoscope which enables us to see past the horse's larynx and down its trachea, or windpipe, has the true incidence of this bleeding been detected. So any horse can have blood draining from a nostril after exercise; it becomes a problem when it happens regularly in the same horse.

Research has shown that the bleeding is caused by abnormal pressures developing in the top part of the lung in tissue which has already been damaged by inflammation during a respiratory virus infection. The problem is more likely to occur in horses which are also suffering from COPD. EIPH is most commonly seen in racehorses because of the extreme pressures put on the respiratory system during the final stages of a race.

Action

Once a horse starts to bleed from the nose regularly, there is little that can be done, because the damage to the lungs which is associated with the condition is permanent. Any measure which reduces co-existing respiratory problems will help to reduce the tension in the upper lung and so reduce the incidence of EIPH. So **a clean air regime should be instituted,** and if necessary brochodilator drugs such as clenbuterol given. There has been considerable publicity for the use of the diuretic frusemide to prevent EIPH. Although its precise action is uncertain, it does reduce the incidence of the problem.

Any co-existing respiratory problems which decrease the airway, such as laryngeal paralysis, should be dealt with if at all possible, so that strain on the respiratory system is reduced.

INFLUENZA

There are two main strains of equine influenza virus, the Type 1 Prague strain and the Type 2 Miami strain. As in human influenza, there are also numerous subtypes of virus, although they do not vary as greatly from the two main types of virus as do the many strains of human influenza.

Equine influenza is a serious respiratory disease which can cause death, especially in foals. It spreads rapidly, with an incubation period of 3-10 days. Affected horses cough frequently, often with a moist cough. They are obviously ill and have a fever. They have a nasal discharge. If the horse is stressed before recovery is complete, the infection may permanently weaken the muscles of the heart. The same circumstances may also predispose the horse to future COPD.

Action

Equine influenza is an unnecessary disease. There are very effective vaccines available which give good protection. It is important to use a vaccine containing the virus strain currently causing clinical disease. Vaccination is compulsory for horses entering many types of competition. **The minimum accepted vaccination requirements are for two primary injections separated by 21-92 days. The first booster should be given 150-210 days afterwards, and annual boosters thereafter.**

There is no treatment to kill the influenza virus. Treatment with mucolytics, such as Sputolosin, and bronchodilators, such as clenbuterol, will reduce the severity of the symptoms and speed up recovery. **Infection should be followed by six weeks complete rest to avoid developing heart problems. The whole yard should be placed in strict isolation** because of the risk of an epidemic being triggered off.

LARYNGEAL PARALYSIS

This refers to a paralysis, partial or complete, of the nerve (the recurrent laryngeal nerve) which supplies the muscles which open the airway through the larynx by pulling aside the vocal cords. Almost invariably it is the nerve on the left side which is affected, and so the left vocal cord which fails to move aside during strenuous exercise. There is considerable air turbulence around the paralysed vocal cord, and this gives rise to a roaring noise when the horse is given strenuous exercise. For this reason the condition is sometimes called 'roaring', but you should be aware that other conditions of the respiratory tract can cause this noise as well as the paralysis which I have described. The horse's larynx must be examined via a fibreoptic endoscope in order to confirm the diagnosis by actually seeing the paralysed vocal cord.

Action
If the horse makes a roaring noise because of laryngeal paralysis, but is still able to fulfill all the athletic demands made of it without showing any respiratory distress,

then no action is necessary. For many years the treatment of this condition was by a surgical operation known as a Hobday operation. This consists of removing a membranous sac from behind the vocal cord. It may reduce the noise in some cases, but it rarely increases the size of the actual airway. If the condition affects the horse's performance significantly, then a tie-back operation is the treatment of choice. This uses Lycra to literally tie the vocal cord back in the position which it should occupy during exercise. The airway is obviously then increased.

LUNGWORM

There is a parasitic worm called *Dictyoculus arnfieldi* which actually lives in the horse's lungs. The adult worms lay eggs which are removed from the lungs with mucus in the usual way and then swallowed. The eggs pass out onto the pasture, where they hatch into larvae. These may then be consumed during grazing, and migrate back to the lungs for the rest of their development. Luckily it is rare for the larvae actually to mature into adult lungworms in the horse. In the vast majority of cases the development stops at the larval stage in the lungs. Most infections in the horse are picked up from eggs laid by lungworms living in donkeys. Unless they have been specifically treated, almost all donkeys are infected with lungworms; but the parasites rarely cause any symptoms in the donkey whereas they almost invariably do so in horses.

In the horse a lungworm infestation causes a chronic cough. It is unusual because the cough often starts during a time of grazing rather than whilst the horse is stabled. The horse may show no other symptoms, although sometimes there is a nasal discharge. In severe cases the breathing can become very laboured. Diagnosis by looking for worm eggs in the faeces is obviously very unreliable. Examination of a sample of mucus from the horse's trachea will usually show the presence of abnormal cells if there is a lungworm infestation. The response to treatment is probably the most reliable way to diagnose the disease.

Action
Remove the horse from any contact with donkeys, and avoid using the paddock for grazing for at least a year. The wormer ivermectin is effective against lungworms at normal dose levels.

STRANGLES

Strangles is an infection of the lymph glands, especially those around the larynx and underneath the jaw. It is caused by a bacterium called *Streptococcus equi*. An affected horse has a raised temperature and a profuse nasty smelling discharge from its nose. The glands around the angle of the jaw can become exceedingly swollen, and in time may burst, releasing thick pus. The horse may have difficulty in breathing. Strangles is usually a disease of young horses, which are often affected as they are mixed and stressed for the first time. It is extremely infectious.

Action
The pus discharging from any burst abscess and from the nose is very infectious. **Strict hygiene is essential** to prevent the spread of the bacteria to other horses by contamination of tack, clothing etc. At certain stages of the disease treatment with antibiotics can be very effective. **Hot fomentations may help to bring the abscesses in the lymph glands to a head quickly.** Bursting of the abscesses is then usually accompanied by a marked improvement in the horse's condition. There are no vaccines against strangles available in the UK.

4 The Circulatory System

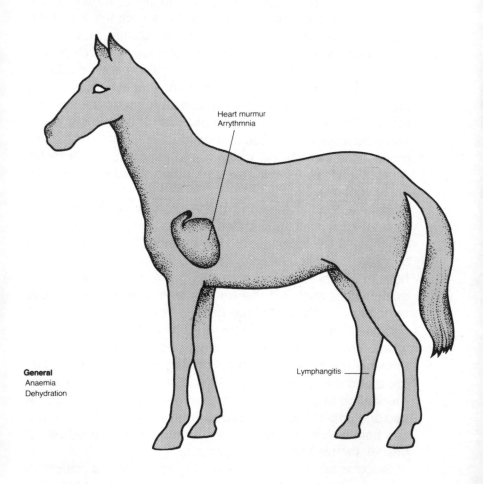

Heart murmur
Arrythmnia

Lymphangitis

General
Anaemia
Dehydration

The circulatory system is one of the miracles of life. The heart pumps away without ever tiring in order to supply to every part of the horse's body, no matter how distant, with the food and oxygen it needs. The heart has four chambers, each of which pumps independently. Blood with very little oxygen in it comes into the right atrium. From there it is pumped into the right ventricle before being sent through the lungs to receive more oxygen. The blood then returns to the left atrium, which pumps it into the right ventricle, and it is from there that the blood is pumped around the general circulation. Having two pumps on each side of the heart is not quite as pointless as it might at first seem. It enables the heart to separate the blood which is returning to the heart from that which is being pumped out of the heart. So if a fault develops in the system, the appropriate pump can compensate. If a ventricle is not pumping as well as it should, the atrium may dilate to accommodate the extra blood which is still returning to the heart, without any such extra pressure being put on the already faulty ventricle.

As everyone knows, the blood vessels which carry the oxygen-rich blood are called arteries, whereas the ones which carry the carbon dioxide-rich blood back towards the heart are the veins. Arteries have muscles in their walls which help to pump the blood along. When a horse is wounded, many people think that an artery has been cut merely because there is a good flow of blood pulsing from the wound. This is not usually the case. If an artery has been severed, the blood will pump a foot or more into the air because of the tremendous pressure under which it is flowing. If a major artery is cut, the blood may spurt many feet across the stable. Whatever the source of bleeding, pressure is the correct treatment. A pad should be held or bandaged firmly over the wound. If you can hold it tight enough for long enough over the actual cut vessel, the bleeding will always stop.

Blood looks red, but is actually made up of a variety of colours. There are the red blood cells, which are present in large numbers (approximately seven million in each millilitre of blood). There are the white blood cells which are present in far fewer numbers (perhaps seven thousand in each millilitre of blood) and there is the straw-coloured fluid, or plasma. The sole role of the red blood cells is to carry oxygen from places where it is abundant, such as the lungs, to the tissues, and there to swop it for carbon dioxide which is carried back to the lungs to be swopped for oxygen again. White blood cells come in a number of different types. They are basically responsible for fighting infection, indeed pus is a mixture of dead white blood cells and bacterial cells. White blood cells not only trap foreign substances and bacteria, they also manufacture antibodies to fight them. Plasma is the carrier mechanism which transports food substances around the body, and toxic waste products which are on their way to be excreted. In this category come certain enzymes which are released from damaged tissues. Finding high levels of these chemicals can help us to diagnose which tissue has been damaged. The water component of plasma holds the balance for the whole body. Too little water, for instance, and the blood will become very viscous and not flow properly, causing circulatory problems.

Normal components of a horse's blood					
Haemoglobin	9.5-15.5 g/dl	White blood		Total Protein	55-67 g/l
Red blood		cells	$6-11 \times 10^9$/l	CPK enzyme	16-49 iu/l
cells	$6-10.5 \times 10^{12}$/l	Neutrophils	$3-6.5 \times 10^9$/l	AST enzyme	105-230 iu/l
Packed cell		Lymphocytes	$2-5 \times 10^9$/l	Bilirubin	1.1-2.5 mg/dl
volume	1.5-1.7	Eosinophils	$0.1-0.5 \times 10^9$/l	Blood urea	3-6.4 mmol/l
		Monocytes	$0.2-1 \times 10^9$/l		
Each laboratory has its own normal values, which may differ from those quoted					

ANAEMIA

Anaemia is a lack of haemoglobin in the horse's blood. Haemoglobin is the red pigment which gives blood its colour and which carries oxygen around the general circulation. All the haemoglobin is contained inside red blood cells, although there is a similar pigment, myoglobin, in muscle. A deficiency of haemoglobin causes a lack of oxygen in the tissues, and so almost all the body systems fail to work as efficiently as they should. In particular, a horse with anaemia is lethargic and dull. It gets tired very quickly during exercise and appears to be out of breath.

Anaemia can occur because of a loss of blood cells, either from a wound or as a result of some chronic disease involving blood loss. It can also occur when the horse has a normal number of red blood cells, but each cell has a reduced quantity of haemoglobin. One reason why this may occur is a shortage of iron in the diet. This is a relatively common cause of anaemia in man but, despite what the advertisers of iron supplements may say, is uncommon in the horse. The horse almost invariably obtains enough iron for its requirements during grazing, and in any case it has a very effective scavenging system to make sure it keeps what iron it has got. It is not possible to look at the mucous membranes of a horse's eye or mouth and diagnose anaemia simply on the basis that the membranes look pale in colour. The levels of haemoglobin have to be very low indeed before the colour of these tissues is reliably altered. A blood sample, on the other hand, will tell you not only how many red blood cells there are, but also how much haemoglobin there is in each cell.

Action

If the red cell count is low, and there is no obvious way in which the horse is losing blood, it may be that the problem stems from a failure to manufacture enough red blood cells. Folic acid deficiency is perhaps the commonest reason for this in stabled horses. **Giving a supplement of folic acid (around 500mg per day) will often return red cell**

manufacture to normal, although it takes at least 30 days for the extra cells to come through into the blood stream. **Iron supplements and vitamin B$_{12}$ supplements do not result in any extra red blood cells being formed.** The horse should also be dosed with ivermectin to make sure that the blood loss is not due to worm larvae damage.

DEHYDRATION

Dehydration is a state where the body has lost a potentially dangerous amount of its body fluids, to the extent that it can no longer compensate for that loss. We often forget that the body consists of 60% water. Various salts, such as sodium, calcium, chloride etc. are dissolved in this fluid in critical concentrations, and dehydration is a serious condition because it affects the levels of these electrolytes which are available to the horse. When the degree of dehydration gets to a really dangerous level, it can be detected by pinching up a fold of skin on the side of the horse's neck or shoulder. When you let go, the fold should immediately slip flat again. If the horse has lost more than 5 per cent of its body weight as fluid, the fold will remain standing.

Dehydration can occur due to loss of fluid and electrolytes during sweating. This may be in response to very hot weather or it may be in response to a need to cool down by sweating after strenuous exercise. Diarrhoea also causes dehydration, indeed dehydration is the major cause of death in diseases which cause diarrhoea, such as salmonellosis.

Action
Both the fluid and the electrolytes must be replaced. If you just give the horse water to drink, that water will be quickly lost from the system again because it does not have enough electrolytes dissolved in it to hold it in the circulation. Equally, merely giving electrolyte powder is no good, you have to give

fluid as well. **There are several proprietary electrolyte mixtures on the market ready to mix with water.** They are very effective, and if your horse is regularly stressed and loses a lot of fluid in sweat, then it is worth having one of these preparations at hand. **A rough guide otherwise is to give the horse 5 litres of water containing 2 tablespoons of table salt for every hour that the horse has been sweating.**

LYMPHANGITIS

Although it does not receive much attention, there is a third part of the circulatory system in addition to the arteries and veins. This is the lymphatic system. It operates in parallel to the veins, draining tissue fluid rather than actual blood, and then returning this fluid into the general circulation. The lymphatic vessels are so thin and small that they are not readily visible, and the pressure of the fluid inside the lymphatics is so low that we can hardly tell that it is there. If, however, the lymphatic drainage becomes blocked, perhaps at one of the lymph nodes which are present at intervals and whose role is to trap any infectious agents present in the lymph and surrounding tissues, then the pressure does build up. When this happens we may be able to see or feel the cord-like lymphatics where they pass under the skin. More often, the pressure forces fluid through the lymphatic walls and out into the surrounding tissues as oedema. The area which should be drained by that particular lymphatic then becomes puffy and swollen. Firm pressure with a finger leaves a pit which remains when the finger is removed. This is lymphangitis.

The commonest place for lymphangitis to occur is in the lower legs, especially the hind legs. Monday Morning Disease is a specific form of lymphangitis where the horse's hind legs are very swollen after a rest day on full rations of food. The oedema makes the legs stiff so the horse is unwilling to move, and this in turn encourages more fluid to accumulate.

Action

Whenever possible **the horse should be given gentle exercise to encourage the general circulation. Cold compresses will help** to limit the amount of new fluid which accumulates and relieve any inflammation in the lymph nodes. Diuretics (drugs which draw fluid out of the body by increasing urine formation) help to reduce the oedema.

MURMURS AND FAULTY RHYTHMS

At rest the horse's heart beats at approximately 40 beats per minute, and if we listen to its regular rhythm we hear at least two heart sounds (often represented as LUB DUB). There are in fact four heart sounds, and in some horses these extra sounds can also be heard. They must not be mistaken for a heart murmur, which is an extra abnormal sound either separating the major heart sounds or between two successive sets of beats. A heart murmur is caused by turbulence in the blood flow. This turbulence may be due to a physical abnormality, such as a faulty heart valve, but it can also be due to an abnormality of the blood and how it flows. So a very anaemic horse may well have a heart murmur, but this is not due to anything wrong with the heart and when the anaemia is cured the murmur disappears.

Faulty heart rhythms, called arrhythmias, are self-explanatory. They are caused by faulty conduction of the electrical impulses in the heart which control the contractions of the various heart chambers. Perhaps the most common arrhythmia is atrial fibrillation, where the top chambers of the heart, the atria, contract repeatedly at a very fast rate which has no relationship with the normal heart rate. Not surprisingly such a horse has very little exercise tolerance.

Anyone can learn to count a horse's heart rate by taking its pulse where the artery curves over the bottom of the lower jaw. Further information comes from listening to the heart with a stethoscope, which gives information about blood flow. The human ear is not sensitive enough to pick up subtle changes in heart rhythms. These are detected using an electrocardiogram (ECG) which uses electrodes fastened to the body to measure the electrical impulses in the heart. The ECG produces a printed trace which enables even small variations in rhythm to be measured. It is also becoming possible actually to see inside the heart as it works, by using an ultra-sound scanner similar to that used to confirm pregnancy in women.

Action

Except in really exceptional circumstances, **no action is necessary** when a heart abnormality is only present at rest and disappears completely as soon as the horse starts exercise. On the other hand, an abnormality which is not present at rest but which appears with exercise will always cause concern. In recent years the veterinary profession has taken a much more lenient view of heart abnormalities than it used to do. The present feeling is that a horse should not be condemned just because of the abnormality, there should be some evidence that the abnormality is having a deleterious effect, eg by reducing the horse's exercise tolerance. Horses with heart problems are unlikely to collapse during exercise. In fact they are, if anything, more likely to collapse when they relax afterwards, but then that is true of people as well. Most heart problems are self-limiting; the horse is incapable of doing more than its heart is able to supply oxygen for.

5 The Locomotor System

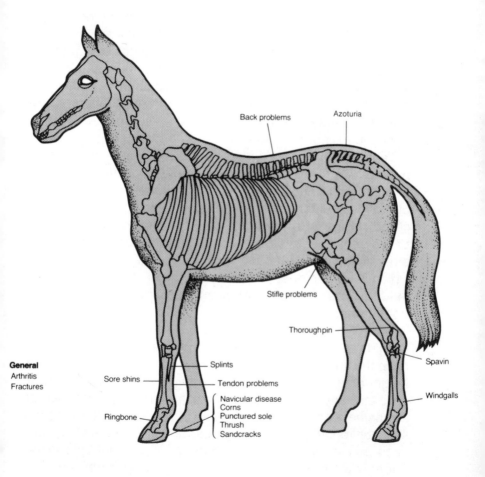

Back problems

Azoturia

Stifle problems

Thoroughpin

Spavin

General
Arthritis
Fractures

Sore shins

Splints

Tendon problems

Navicular disease
Corns
Punctured sole
Thrush
Sandcracks

Ringbone

Windgalls

The musculo-skeletal system consists of the muscles of the body which are under conscious control, the tendons which attach them to bones, the bones themselves and the ligaments which join certain bones together. The bony skeleton forms a system of levers for propelling the horse along, and the muscles move those levers.

Muscle is an extremely active tissue. It always has a very good blood supply in order to bring oxygen and food to the muscle and to remove waste products. When a muscle is injured, this blood supply is a positive advantage, because it brings all the building blocks needed to repair the damaged tissue. So muscles heal quickly and completely within a matter of weeks as long as they are not subjected to further injury. Every muscle has an opponent, another muscle which pulls on the same bone but in the opposite direction. Controlled movement is a balance between the pull exerted by these opposing muscles.

Tendon is a relatively inactive tissue. Despite what some people think, it does have a reasonable blood supply considering the small number of active cells present in tendon. Most of the mass of tendon is made up of large fibres of a protein called collagen. Normal tendon collagen fibres have a 'crimp', or zig-zag, pattern which allows them a certain amount of stretching. When a tendon injury heals initially, the collagen which is formed does not have this crimp, and so the healed tendon does not have that slight elasticity which protects it from further damage.

Bone is not the completely inactive tissue that many people imagine. It is true that the shape and size of bones alters little once the horse is mature. In fact horses grow relatively little in height after they are two of three years old. Bone has fewer cells than any other tissue; most of it is made up of crystals of a substance called hydroxy apatite. This substance is responsible for keeping the levels of important minerals in the blood, such as calcium and phosphorus, at a constant safe level. There is a continuous turnover of mineral, with new crystals being formed and others broken down. If the blood calcium levels start to go down, the rate, at which new apatite crystals are formed is automatically reduced until enough calcium has accumulated in the blood. If the blood calcium levels are getting too high, the rate of apatite breakdown is reduced. We think of minerals such as calcium and phosphorus as being primarily essential in the horse's diet to make healthy bone, but they have many other, equally important, roles in the body's general metabolism.

Ligaments are very like tendons in structure, except that they contain more elastic fibres. Their role is to hold bones together at joints, allowing the bones to move in certain directions but perhaps not in others. A joint is a rather complex system. The adjoining bones have to have a covering of cartilage to allow them to move smoothly over each other without friction and wear. As I have mentioned, the bones are often held in place by ligaments. The whole joint is lubricated by joint fluid, which also keeps alive the cartilage, and this fluid is kept in place by a joint capsule. Inflammation of the joint, from whatever cause, usually results in an increase in the amount of joint fluid produced by the joint capsule, and the increased activity may be felt as heat around the joint. Much of the pain associated with joint problems stems from the fact that the joint fluid manufactured at that time is not as good a lubricant as it should be.

Tendons, bones, ligaments and joint capsules do not have a very well developed defence system against infection. So if, despite their relative inactivity, an infection does manage to establish itself, it can have dramatic results. The same situation applies to the sheaths which surround the major tendons such as those down the back of the cannon bone.

Diagnosis of lameness
1 Have the horse trotted away from you in hand. Observe any sinking of the hind quarters.
2 Have the horse trotted towards you in hand. Observe any nodding of the head.
3 The horse sinks or nods on the **sound** leg, and so is lame on the other leg.
4 Examine the leg for any heat, swelling or pain.
5 Remember that 90% of lameness is in the foot anyway.

ARTHRITIS (DEGENERATIVE JOINT DISEASE – DJD)

Arthritis means inflammation of a joint. It has come to imply that permanent damage has been caused to the joint, which is painful to the horse. Navicular disease, ringbone and spavin are all examples of arthritis which will be dealt with individually below. In man rheumatoid arthritis is relatively common. In the horse it is extremely rare.

Every joint in the body is potentially a site of arthritis. In most cases this arises because of wear and tear on the joint surfaces, and so arthritis is most common in horses which have been very active athletically and in older horses. Besides being painful, affected joints are often swollen because of an increase in the amount of joint fluid present. They may also be warm to the touch. On X-ray the characteristic finding is that new bone has been formed around the arthritic joint. Sometimes small fragments of bone break off into the joint fluid. These are referred to as joint mice.

Action
Any joint which is painful for more than a day or two should be viewed as possibly having an arthritis. It is important to know exactly what you are dealing with, and so X-rays are an essential part of the diagnosis. If, for example, the problem is just a sprain of the ligaments around a joint then cold compresses, laser therapy, and possibly anti-inflammatory drugs will usually do the trick. If there is a fragment of bone loose in the joint cavity, such treatment might be pointless until the fragment has been removed surgically. Whatever the cause of a joint swelling, the first and most important part of any treatment is rest.

Anti-inflammatory drugs, such as phenylbutazone, flunixen or meclofenamic acid, do not heal arthritis. They merely take the pain away. So their use is almost certainly going to have to be permanent if the affected horse is to remain in work. Recently it has been appreciated that inflammation of the joint cartilage is responsible for more of the pain than the actual bony changes. This in turn results in changes in the joint fluid which make it a much less efficient lubricant. Replacing this faulty joint fluid with either healthy fluid from another joint on the same horse, or, more usually, with an articifial product, can give a tremendous amount of relief. Polysulphated glycosaminoglycans protect the inflamed cartilage.

AZOTURIA

This condition has a variety of names, including setfast and exertional rhabdomyelosis. The clinical symptoms are easy to describe; their cause can be more difficult to unravel. In acute azoturia the horse starts to stiffen up during exercise. The large muscle masses of the back and hind quarters become hard and painful. If the horse is forced to keep on exercising, the condition can deteriorate to the point where the horse is unable to move at all. The horse may then become recumbent, and unable to get back on its feet. A horse with azoturia may be seen to strain as it tries unsuccessfully to pass urine. If any urine is passed it may be very dark, almost reddish, in colour. Acute azoturia usually occurs on the first or second day of exercise following a short rest period when the horse was still fed full concentrate rations.

Subclinical azoturia shows as a horse which sweats far more readily during exercise than one would expect. It can canter and gallop, but does not perform as well as expected, and may breathe more heavily than expected for the amount of work it has done.

Azoturia should be looked upon as an abnormal form of fatigue. When a horse is tired, the weakness and pain it feels in its muscles are due to the accumulation of large amounts of lactic acid which have not been removed by the circulation. In azoturia large amounts of lactic acid also accumulate and these cause severe muscle damage because of their acidity. This muscle damage can be assessed by measuring the levels of certain enzymes which have escaped from the damaged cells into the blood. There is often no obvious reason why the lactic acid has been formed in such large quantities. If the horse has been over-fed for the amount of exercise it has done, then the excess carbohydrate will have been stored in the muscles as the starch, glycogen. When this is broken down to release energy, large amounts of lactic acid may be formed. In horses which develop azoturia when they have not been rested, or where they have been on only a low plane of nutrition, the triggering factor is less obvious. Some horses do not absorb enough electrolytes, such as sodium, to produce stable muscle cell walls and these are then more easily damaged than would otherwise be expected.

Action

If you suspect that your horse is developing azoturia, do not go any further. If you are any great distance from your base, do not attempt to get back but arrange temporary accommodation. Experience after long-distance rides has shown that even the need to brace itself during transport in a horsebox can make a horse's condition worse. **With the exception of one or two short (3 or 4 minutes maximum) daily walks in hand, the horse should be rested until the muscle enzyme levels have returned to normal.** Many horses which are said to be prone to azoturia are nothing of the sort, it is just that they are never allowed to recover completely before being returned to work, and so are permanently subclinical cases.

In acute azoturia the horse should be discouraged from lying down because the great effort needed to get a horse to its feet will at best make the situation worse. In some cases, once the muscles have stiffened up whilst the horse is lying down, they cannot raise the horse at all.

Breakdown products from the muscles clog up the kidneys in azoturia, and so **horses should be encouraged to drink and pass urine** in order to wash these substances away. Diuretic drugs may be given to help wash out the kidneys. Intravenous fluid infusions can do the same thing. As there is muscle damage, anti-inflammatory drugs such as cortisone are useful.

Vitamin E and selenium may speed up the recovery of the muscles after an attack of azoturia. Attempts to prove this scientifically have not always been successful, but there is nothing to lose by their use. Specific electrolyte mixtures are now being used to stabilise the muscle membranes. **1oz of salt per day is a good basic supplement for any horse considered at risk.**

BACK PROBLEMS

Back trouble is a very common diagnosis for horse owners to make. This helped by the fact that there are a number of unqualified itinerant back 'manipulators' who will diagnose and treat back problems by manipulation although they know nothing about any other disease process or treatment. It is also helped by the fact that one of the commonest symptoms of back pain is loss of performance, and this happens all too often in athletic horses. A distinction must be made between muscle spasm of the back muscles (the longissimus dorsi and the gluteal muscles) which is a primary problem due to injury, and spasm which is the result of the horse attempting to redistribute its weight because of some other primary problem. Treatment of the latter situation may give temporary relief, but the problem will re-occur if the primary problem, such as a bony abnormality of the spine or a chronic foot lameness, is not dealt with first.

Diagnosis of a muscular back problem starts with careful pressure along the back muscles. It is interesting that there are certain spots where any pain appears to be most marked, and these are also acupuncture 'points'. It is not normal for any horse to shrink away from pressure on a particular spot. A horse with a 'cold' back is a horse which either has a problem now or remembers a past problem. The critical point is whether by treatment it is possible to switch off this reaction, thus proving that there really was pain there all the time. Careful observation of the back may reveal muscles which have wasted because of lack of use. In cases of recent muscle injury, the muscle enzymes in the blood may be increased.

Back muscle pain can be due to actual tearing of the muscles as a result of a fall or an awkward movement. The owner may not be aware of this because horses often roll, and even get cast, in their boxes at night. The pain may also be due to muscle spasm; the muscle fibres along a short length of the back go into a continuous contraction. They can stay contracted like this for long periods, causing a focus of pain as they become exhausted but still fail to relax.

Bony problems of the back are more difficult to diagnose, despite the desire of manipulators to persuade us that they are manipulating bones rather than relieving muscle spasms. Pressure on the dorsal spines of the vertebrae may reveal pain, and injecting local anaesthetic between adjacent spines may complete the diagnosis by removing that pain. X-ray examination of the spine and pelvis unfortunately requires a high-powered machine which is only likely to be available in research clinics etc. The commonest bony problem is kissing, or rubbing, of adjacent dorsal spines. Surveys show that this is a relatively common occurrence, and usually appears to cause no problems. In occasional horses, however, the new bone formation is so great and painful that the horse has obvious symptoms of pain. Nuclear scintigraphy, which shows 'hot spots' of bone activity, may locate the site of active bony problems.

Action

Most back problems can be cured by six months rest in the stable. In the majority of cases this is not feasible or appropriate. Nevertheless, **rest is an important part of treatment**. If you continue to ask a horse with a back problem to jump or perform dressage, you will keep the problem active.

Anti-inflammatory drugs can be very useful in relieving the pain of back problems, but such artificial relief should never be used merely to enable the horse to continue working, and so possibly aggravating the condition. In addition to the usual drugs of this kind, such as phenylbutazone, naproxen is specifically useful in muscle problems.

I have already mentioned manipulation of horses backs. Different operators perform this in different ways, be it by pushing, hitting or twisting. **The end result of manipulation is to relieve muscle pain rather than move bones.** This can be proved by the fact that treatment of the same point along the back with other forms of therapy, such as lasers, will give the same relief but can obviously not have moved any structural part of the anatomy. Manipulation can be a valuable tool in providing temporary pain relief, and also in diagnosis of back problems. It would undoubtedly be more widely used if people were not put off by the extravagant claims associated with it.

Laser therapy of the back uses a laser emitting light in the infra-red spectrum. It is true that such lasers can excite acupuncture points, but with back problems it is more likely that it is the anti-inflammatory effect which is more important. This is achieved by raising circulatory levels of natural anti-inflammatory hormones such as cortisol and seratonin. The results, from the point of view of switching off back pain, can be dramatic. It is also painless, and so does not cause the tensing of the back muscles seen in horses which have received previous manipulation of their back.

Faradism is another way of treating muscle problems. An electrical current is set up between one electrode located in a surcingle, and another electrode which is held on the skin over the injured area. The current is pulsed to cause regular contraction and relaxation of the stimulated muscles. This helps the circulation to remove inflammatory fluids, and also builds up the muscle by providing exercise without load-bearing to undo the healing. We do not know how deep the contractions are which are stimulated by faradism. It may only be the superficial muscles which are affected. Care must be taken with faradism not to stimulate the muscles too strongly, as this may cause tearing of only partially recovered fibres.

Massage may help to relax the muscles of the back which are in spasm. Effective manual massage is difficult to achieve with large muscles like those along the horse's back, but there are some effective machines such as the Niagara therapy pads which will achieve a similar or even better effect.

Bony back problems do require long periods of rest. In this case, I certainly do mean 6 months box rest. If this is not successful, surgery may be the only alternative.

CORNS

A corn is an area of bruised sole underneath the last inch or so of either heel of the shoe. The bruising is caused by a combination of a poorly fitting shoe and weight being borne by the back of the foot rather than its centre. Corns are commonest on the front feet, and on the inside heel of the foot, because this is where most of the weight comes to press.

A corn causes a chronic lameness, which initially may be difficult to spot. The foot remains cool to the touch, and because the area is covered by the shoe there is nothing to see. Squeezing the appropriate part of the foot with hoof testers may cause pain, but the real diagnosis rests with seeing the actual corn once the shoe has been removed. Only when this has been done, and the top layers of horn have been removed, can the damp, pink bruising be detected on the sole. If an infection is present, pus (possibly black in colour like so much pus in horn) will replace the bloody tissue fluid normally associated with a corn.

Action
Corns should be considered as the possible cause of any chronic foot lameness. The shoe will have been removed during their diagnosis, and it should be left off for a few days to allow the underlying sensitive laminae of the foot to recover. **The bruised or infected horn should be cut away.** Poulticing may then help to reduce the pain and inflammation. **The horse should be reshod with a properly fitting shoe that is cut away on the ground surface for the first inch**

from each affected heel. This means that less pressure is put on the seat of the corn as the horse exercises.

Prevention of corns is based on employing a good farrier to shoe the horse, and having him do this at frequent intervals. Some horses are said to be particularly prone to corns. In most cases this can be traced back to the shape of the foot, its shoeing or the long length of time between shoeings.

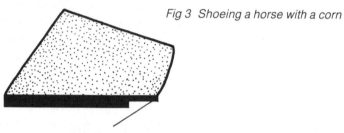

Fig 3 Shoeing a horse with a corn

weight-bearing surface of the shoe
cut away over the heel which has the corn

FRACTURES

A fracture is a broken bone. Obviously, any bone in the body can be broken, but fractures of the legs are probably the most common because of the immense forces of leverage exerted during movement. The most important symptoms of a fracture are sudden pain and abnormal movement. So if a horse is unwilling to use a part of the body at all, then it may be that the severe pain is due to a fracture. Similarly, when a bone is broken, the two or more fragments will often be pulled in different directions, especially if the horse tries to bear weight on the broken bone. So a broken bone may appear to be an unusual shape. Swelling may appear around the site of the fracture. A bone does not fracture over a number of days, so a problem which starts as a minor problem and steadily deteriorates is probably not a fracture.

Action

From the first-aid point of view, it is better to suspect too many fractures than too few. A sudden onset of swelling and acute pain connected with a bone should be treated as a fracture until proved otherwise. **The essential thing is to immobilise the limb. The materials for a Robert Jones splint should be in your first aid kit.** The splint consists of at least two, and preferably three large rolls (approximately 500g weight) of cotton wool or gamgee being wrapped around the leg. This is then held in place by a bandage applied as tightly as possible. Veterinary help should be summoned after you have applied the splint, not before. A considerable amount of extra damage can be caused at a fracture site if the broken bones are allowed to move and grate on each other for even a few minutes.

Many fractures of the lower limbs can now be mended quite satisfactorily by surgery. Fractures of the upper limbs still present a problem and may result in euthanasia for the horse.

NAVICULAR DISEASE

It has been said that navicular disease is the commonest cause of chronic lameness in the horse. The lameness often affects both front feet. If they are both equally affected, the horse may not appear lame at all, but merely have a short stride and a pottery gait. More often the horse is lame on one leg, but this is merely the foot which has the most pain. If the foot is nerve-blocked to remove the pain, the horse immediately shows a lameness in the other foot. There is usually no outward sign of navicular disease. Sometimes a severely affected foot may become contracted at the heels, which is why one should be suspicious of buying a horse with one foot a different size from the other, but in the majority of cases the feet look identical. There is no heat in the foot, nor is there any pain if you hammer or squeeze the foot.

The lameness often appears gradually. In the early stages

of navicular disease the horse may only be lame for a few strides when it is first brought out of the stable after rest. Other cases are only lame on occasional days. As the condition progresses though, the horse becomes permanently lame. Navicular disease tends to improve temporarily following a few days rest, but to be exacerbated by 30-40 minutes rest after strenuous exercise.

At the present time there is considerable international controversy over the cause of the symptoms which we call navicular disease. It would appear that there are a number of changes in the foot which give the same symptoms, and a number of ways in which such changes can be triggered off. The name 'navicular disease' stems from the fact that post-mortem examinations of affected horses years ago showed erosions on the cartilage covering the navicular bone. This was strengthened by the finding of X-ray changes in the bone. In recent years more attention has been focussed on the foot as a whole being involved. In particular, the blood supply is involved. Many of the small blood vessels in the navicular bone become blocked by clotted blood in clinical cases, and this is thought to be due to poor blood pressure and circulation through the foot. Measurements have shown that in clinical cases much of the blood which is intended for the foot shunts around the coronet and then goes back up the leg without ever going into the foot at all, so that there is pooling of the slow moving blood in the foot.

Diagnosis of navicular disease requires the presence of a number of features. The horse must be chronically lame, with the lameness located in the foot by nerve-blocks. In addition, there must be X-ray changes in the navicular bone of the affected foot. Most of these changes reflect an attempt to increase the blood supply to the bone by increasing the number and distribution of the nutrient foramen, the holes where the blood vessels enter the bone, but other changes are also seen. It is unsafe to make a diagnosis purely on clinical grounds, just as it is unsafe to make one simply on the presence of X-ray changes in an otherwise sound horse. Many horses with navicular disease become markedly lame for a few strides after carrying out a 'flexion test' even before clinical lameness has developed. Ths test is carried out by holding the foot so as to flex, or bend, the fetlock joint backwards as much as possible. After about thirty seconds the foot is released and the horse immediately trotted off.

Opinions vary as to whether navicular disease is hereditary or not. The high incidence in certain breeding lines and certain breeds, such as the Thoroughbred and Thoroughbred crosses, may reflect conformation tendencies. A long toe and short heel, producing a 'broken foot/pastern axis', plays a large part in the development of the disease. Again this may be due to the fact that it results in extra weight being borne by the heel of the foot, which is less rigid. This in turn may result in constriction of the blood vessels.

Action

We have fortunately moved a long way from the times when the diagnosis of navicular disease signed a horse's death warrant. **The first step is to get the feet of an affected horse properly trimmed and balanced.** If you do not do this, the horse will not respond to anything else. The second step is to shoe the horse sensibly. Most authorities favour the use of an oval-shaped shoe to support the heels, but **shoeing with a normal shoe, but placed slightly back from the toe and extending back behind the heels may be sufficient as long as it has a rolled toe.** The third step is to persuade your farrier to keep the foot like this, and not slip back into bad habits over the succeeding months.

Treatment to increase the blood supply has been very successful for navicular disease. The original drug used was warfarin. This has the disadvantage that it is extremely toxic because it delays blood clotting and so increases the risk of fatal haemorrhage from quite ordinary wounds. Regular six-weeks blood checks are necessary to monitor the amount of the drug which can be given safely. Isoxsuprine is now widely used as a dilator of the small blood vessels in the foot. This enables the blood to flow more freely. This drug is non-toxic. Treatment lasts for about 12 weeks. Both drugs are given by

Figs 4-6 Shoeing for navicular disease. It is essential that horses with navicular disease have a properly balance foot

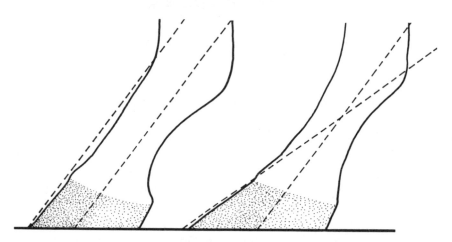

Fig 4 The hoof-pastern axis. Notice how a line drawn up the front of the hoof should be parallel to a line drawn down the centre of the pastern. When the toe is too long the two lines converge, and the weight of the leg is thrown towards the heel rather than the centre of the hoof

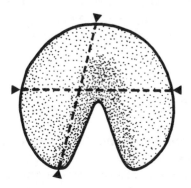

Fig 5 The balanced foot. A line drawn from the middle of the toe to the corner of the heel is exactly the same length as a line drawn across the widest part of the foot

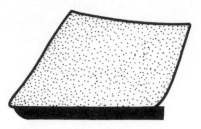

Fig 6 *Lateral view of a foot shod for navicular disease. Notice how the rolled toe is set very slightly back from the toe of the hoof, whilst the heels of the shoe similarly extend fractionally back behind the hoof*

mouth, and their supporters claim that 60-70 per cent of horses treated will return to normal work, at least initially.

You will notice that I have not so far mentioned the use of the painkiller phenylbutazone in the treatment of navicular disease. This is because it is not a treatment at all, merely a masking agent. Horses go sound, but will become lame again as soon as the drug is withdrawn. If a horse is worked while it is kept sound by the use of phenylbutazone, then the condition will continue to deteriorate. Denerving, which consists of cutting the nerve that supplies the foot as it travels down the cannon, also masks an increasing condition rather than improving it.

It has been suggested that surgically cutting the two collateral ligaments which hold the navicular bone tightly in place allows more freedom and leads to a cure even in horses which have not responded to drug treatment.

PUNCTURED SOLE

This is perhaps one of the most dramatic of lamenesses, yet also one of the easiest to cure with proper treatment. The horse becomes increasingly lame over one or two days after it has, usually unbeknown to its owner, trodden on a sharp flint, nail etc. In acute cases the horse will be unwilling to put its foot to the ground at all. If it does do so, it will walk just on the toe rather than putting the flat of the sole down. The foot may be obviously warm to the touch, although you should not be misled if it feels more or less the same temperature as its opposite number. Squeezing the foot with a hoof tester, or hitting it with a hammer, will be obviously painful over the affected area.

It is important to find where the hoof was punctured. A really careful examination of the cleaned sole will almost always reveal a black mark on the sole which is present right through the thickness of the sole rather than just being a superficial mark which disappears when the surface layers are scraped off. Your farrier or veterinary surgeon will follow this trace down until the abscess is reached. The pus will not look the same as in a skin abscess. It will be black or grey in colour, and may be more like a paste or powder than a liquid. It is not sufficient merely to confirm that pus is present, the hole must be made large enough for proper drainage to take place.

Action

The foot should be actively poulticed, ie poulticed at least twice a day, until no more pus has been drawn out for two days. A kaolin or Animalintex poultice is best. Bran poultices have very little effect. If you stop poulticing too early, more pus will accumulate and the horse will go lame again. When you do stop, care must be taken to prevent more infection gaining entry via the hole you have made. So the cavity should be plugged with cotton wool dipped in Stockholm tar or a suitable antibiotic. It may be necessary to put a light pad across the sole in order to keep this plug in place during the first couple of weeks. It may also be advisable to give the horse a course of antibiotic anyway to kill off any infection trying to reach the blood stream.

If the horse is not sound within 3-4 days, the foot must be checked to ensure that drainage can still take place. It may be necessary to flush the abscess with metronidazole or hydrogen peroxide. If the lameness still persists, then obviously the foot must be X-rayed to check for foreign bodies.

SANDCRACK

A sandcrack is a vertical crack in the outer layers of the hoof. The crack may start at the ground, weight-bearing surface of the foot and extend upwards towards the coronet, or it may start at the coronet and extend downwards. In the case of the former, the crack is usually due to the stresses of weight bearing in an over-long foot or the result of poor quality horn. In the case of sandcracks starting from the coronet, the cause is usually an injury to the coronet which has damaged the horn forming tissue.

Many sandcracks do not cause any lameness. The deeper the crack and the further it extends, the more likely it is to weaken the hoof wall and make it unstable during weight bearing. Abnormal pressure is then put on the underlying sensitive laminae, and the horse starts to feel pain. If an infection becomes established in the crack, helped by the fact that the inner layers of horn are not waterproof and so become softened by moisture, this can also make the horse lame.

Action

The crack must be stabilised if it is not to become self-perpetuating due to the stresses of weight bearing. **Grooves in the hoof, either horizontally across the top of the sandcrack or vertically on either side of it, disperse the shearing forces in the hoof wall and prevent further spread.** Unfortunately, in many cases these grooves are not made deep enough and so prove unsuccessful. The groove must be at least as deep as the crack you are dealing with. Nails placed horizontally can help stabilise the crack. A well fitted shoe, perhaps with a clip on either side of the crack, also provides considerable stability.

Any infected horn must be cut away from the depths of the crack. Large cracks can then be stabilised by filling with a synthetic horn replacement paste.

Obviously feet should never be left to grow too long as this predisposes to cracking. **If poor quality horn is suspected**

as a contributory factor, then it is advisable to feed a methionine and/or biotin supplement. These are said to strengthen the bonds between the horn tubules.

SORE SHINS

Although sore shins are most commonly a problem of young immature Thoroughbreds in training, they can affect other types and age of horse. As the name implies, the immature bone down the front of the cannon becomes sore due to the effect of stress from repeated percussion during exercise. The shin may be obviously warm to the touch. The horse may not actually go lame, but will shorten its stride markedly.

Action
The work load should be immediately reduced until the pain disappears. In severe cases, pulsing electromagnetic therapy may help the bone to settle down. Where available, a cortisone/DMSO paint may be applied to the affected shin to reduce the inflammation.

SPAVIN

Spavin is an osteo-arthritis of the lower hock joints. These are joints which are not involved in the normal movement of the hock, but exist between the small bones of the hock to increase its shock-absorbing capabilities. Like most arthritis, spavin is commonest in older horses. Usually the condition affects only one leg. The lameness develops gradually, often increasing at times of heavy work. It is possible to have spavin without any exterior change in the hock. The bony swelling which used to be seen on the inside of the hock in draught horses with spavin is rarely seen nowadays because we rarely allow the condition to progress that far. It is also possible to have quite marked bony changes established before any lameness becomes apparent.

The classic way to diagnose spavin is to perform the spavin test. This consists of holding the hind leg up so that the hock is fully flexed for 1-2 minutes. The leg is then released and the horse immediately trotted off. If the horse is made more lame by this test, or if it makes a previously sound horse lame for the first few strides, then the test is positive. You should be aware, however, that other conditions can also cause a positive test, because other parts of the leg are also being flexed at the same time.

Confirmation of the existence of spavin follows seeing on an X-ray the bony changes, including new bone formation, which develop around the edges of the joints.

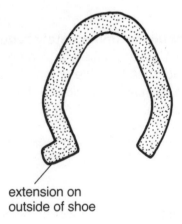

Fig 7 Shoe for spavin

extension on
outside of shoe

Action

With rest an affected horse may become sound, but the lameness will re-occur when the horse starts to be worked again. Phenylbutazone will usually remove the pain, but that is not actually curing the condition. Both the pain and the lameness will go if there is sufficient new bone growth to fuse the affected joints completely. So **the best course of action is to continue gentle work for five or six months in the hope of stimulating more new bone growth, and hopefully fu-**

sion of the joints. **During this time the horse can be kept sound by the use of phenylbutazone.**

Horses with spavin carry the affected leg further underneath the body than normal, and this increases the stress on the joint as well as the pain. **The use of a special shoe which has a short extra length of metal protruding out from the side of the heel of the shoe on the outside, will help to encourage the horse to use its leg normally** and not put the extra strain on the hock which the abnormal action causes. It is surprising how much of an improvement such shoeing can bring about. The horse will need to be shod in this way as a long-term measure.

If the spavin does not respond, and the horse is still lame, the joints can be fused surgically. Once this has happened, the majority of horses become sound.

SPLINTS

A splint is a lump of new bone which is formed at any point down the junction between one of the splint bones and the cannon bone. Splints can occur on either side of the leg (because there is a splint bone on either side) and on both front and back legs. They are extremely common, indeed the majority of horses will have at least one splint present. In the long term they do not usually cause any lameness, although they may do so initially before and during their formation.

It is thought that splints reflect the horse's attempt to strengthen the wall of the cannon bone where possibly immature or over-stressed bone is weak. Splints commonly start to be formed when a young horse first starts work, but they can be formed at any age if the right circumstances arise. Other triggering factors include a kick or blow, and faulty conformation which results in the weight being transmitted more to one side of the leg than the other.

The new bone is formed by the periosteum, or surface layer, of the cannon bone. Much of the initial swelling is

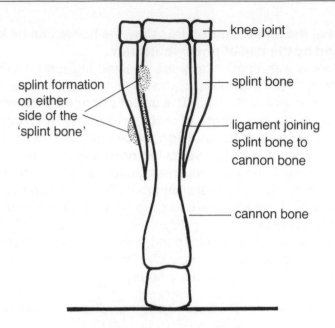

Fig 8 Splint formation in the horse

fibrous tissue, which then becomes ossified. When people talk of a splint having got smaller, this is not because the bone has gone away, but because not all of the original fibrous tissue has been ossified. Sometimes quite large splints can appear very quickly without any pain. In other cases the formation of very small splints can be extremely painful.

For a splint to be implicated as the cause of lameness, it must be painful to firm pressure, and the lameness should disappear if a local anaesthetic is injected around the splint. Often the tissues over the split are warm and swollen during the splint formation.

Action

Cold applications, such as ice packs, will reduce the pain and inflammation sometimes associated with splint formation. Cortisone injections into the area or cortisone-DMSO paint are also used. Chronically painful splints may respond to pulsing electromagnetic therapy to help normal bone formation. If the pain persists more than 10-14 days, it is important that the leg is X-rayed in order to eliminate the possibility of a fracture (possibly incomplete) of the splint bone.

STIFLE PROBLEMS

The stifle joint is the horse's equivalent of our knee joint. It is therefore quite a complicated joint because there is the movement of the patella, or knee-cap, to consider. The horse also has the additional complication of needing to be able to lock its hind legs so that it can sleep standing up. It does this by locking its stifle. To do this, the patella is hooked over a protuberance of bone at the bottom of the femur, thus preventing any movement. In the normal horse this only happens when the horse is actually resting, but the patella can be retained in this position at other times. If the horse is completely unable to pull the patella off the protuberance, then the leg will remain completely straight. Such a horse is said to have 'put its stifle out.' If the horse can move at all, it will drag this rigid leg behind it. More commonly the stifle catches in this position temporarily at the end of every stride, when the leg is straight out behind the body. As the leg is pulled forward, it suddenly frees itself and there is a jerk in its movement. Temporary retention of the patella is most likely to occur as the horse goes around a corner with the affected leg on the outside. It may also occur as the horse moves off at the trot from a standing start.

Usually only one leg is affected with this condition because it is usually brought about by injury to the ligaments which control the patella. The injury may occur in a stable, perhaps when the horse kicks out behind against a wall, or out at exercise. Some horses are thought to have a genetic predisposition to the condition because the ligaments running from the patella are not attached to quite the right place on the bone below the stifle. If a horse or pony is in poor bodily condition, the ligaments may contract slightly, and this may be enough to cause the patella to start catching. The stifle joint is not swollen or warm to the touch with this condition. Only when the horse moves can you feel anything wrong.

Young Thoroughbreds and similar horses may develop a bone cyst in the stifle, which may or may not cause lameness, depending on how hard the horse is trained before the bone becomes fully mature. There is also a specific arthritis of the stifle joint called osteochondritis dessicans. This causes a sudden onset of lameness, with the joint capsule of the stifle obviously swollen with fluid. Some stifle lamenesses give a positive reaction to the spavin test, which can make their diagnosis difficult.

Action

If a horse's stifle locks whilst it is out at exercise, **dismount and try and get the horse to relax as much as possible. Gentle rubbing of the whole stifle area may eventually dislodge the patella and enable the horse to start moving again.** If you cannot free it, arrange transport home and seek veterinary assistance. The horse will need rest and anti-inflammatory drugs to allow the ligaments to return to normal if possible.

In some cases the condition continues to re-occur. Surgery may be the only answer for such horses. The ligament which holds the patella locked in position is cut surgically and then allowed to heal. The resulting scar between the cut ends lengthens the ligament and so prevents the problem re-occurring.

TENDON SPRAINS

When we talk of a sprained tendon, we are referring to the tendons which run down the back of the cannon bones, the superficial and deep flexor tendons. Sprains of the check ligament just below the knee, and the suspensory ligament immediately behind the lower cannon bone, will produce similar symptoms. The tendons of the front legs are usually the ones affected because they are subjected to the greatest stress during galloping and jumping. A sprain occurs during exercise due to a sudden pull on the tendon fibres which exceeds their tensile strength and so causes tearing of the fibres. The classic signs of such an injury are the presence of heat, swelling and pain. The pain will become apparent very shortly after the injury, but the warmth and swelling may take several hours to reach their peak. With the development of an ability to look inside the tendons with an ultra-sound scanner, we have discovered that the amount of pain, heat and swelling which is present during the initial few days does not necessarily bear any relationship to the amount of physical damage caused to the tendon.

Even in acute cases the heat and the worst of the swelling will subside over a period of 2-3 weeks. This leaves a tendon which may be as much as twice its normal cross-sectional area. In time the horse appears to become sound at the walk, and then at the trot, but if it returns to regular work too soon,

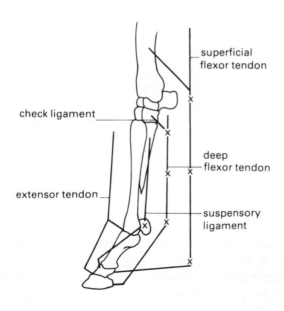

Fig 8a Common sites of tendon strains

the leg returns to its original swollen condition. Occasionally the tendon may be so severely damaged that it is torn completely in two. If this happens, in addition to the local symptoms, the fetlock may sink right down to the ground.

Action

Despite the sudden onset of a strained tendon, and the obvious symptoms, there appears to be an unwillingness on the part of horse owners to treat it as an emergency. Veterinary help should be sought immediately, not when the strain is a couple of weeks old. The administration of cortisone and a diuretic may be able to prevent much of the swelling ever occurring, and so prevent many of the adhesions between skin, tendon sheath and tendon which will otherwise form. **Cold is the vital part of first aid for tendon injuries** because it reduces the blood supply to the area, and it is the blood which brings the inflammatory reaction. Ice packs will need to be replaced every couple of hours because it is amazing how quickly they are heated up by the sprain. Packets of frozen peas may make a more manageable ice pack than lumps of ice out of a fridge. Purpose-made packs and frozen bandages are available. At the same time, **firm support will limit the amount of swelling.** Care must be taken though not to bandage tendons too tightly. Even healthy tendons can be damaged by too tight bandaging. Sodium hyaluronate appears to reduce the inflammation and give better healing of the tendon.

During the initial inflammatory reaction, laser therapy may help to reduce swelling. It is important to realise that healing will still have to take place within the tendon, and the horse is not necessarily ready to return to work just because the swelling has decreased after treatment. Scientific studies have shown that blistering and firing of tendons does not speed up their healing at all, and may delay it. **In all cases rest is essential.** During the initial couple of weeks when there is heat in the tendon, this should be complete stable rest. Afterwards the horse can be walked out in hand for 10-15 minutes twice a day. The length of time the horse will be off work varies from 3 weeks when there is only heat in the tendon, to 9-12 months when the tendon is very hot and swollen and the horse is lame even at the walk. **Ultra-sound scanning will show when the tendon has fully healed, and so is able to stand work.**

THOROUGHPIN

Thoroughpin is a tenosynovitis of the sheath of the deep flexor tendon just above the hock. It is recognised by a cold painless swelling just below the Achilles tendon above the hock joint. It is not associated with any lameness, although it is thought to be a response to repeated trauma, possibly made worse by poor conformation. The swelling may decrease slightly with exercise.

Action
No action is necessary as it is simply a blemish. **Bandaging during rest may limit the swelling.** Removal of the fluid and injecting cortisone into the sheath may give a temporary improvement.

THRUSH

Thrush is an infection of the horn. It usually involves the softer horn of the frog, but other parts of the hoof can be affected. The horn becomes black and has a foul-smelling odour. It is softened by the infection,and may look wet and slimy. Especially when the infection affects the deep cracks around the frog, thrush can make a horse lame.

Thrush can become more easily established in horn which has been softened by constant exposure to moisture such as water or urine. It is therefore most commonly seen in horses kept in dirty stables on damp bedding, or horses standing outside in a great deal of mud. Because of this environmental predisposition, thrush can affect more than one foot at the same time.

Action

The first step is to improve the hygiene so that the horn of the hoof can dry out and remain dry and healthy. **All the affected horn should be cut away. Dilute formalin solution makes a good thrush dressing.** It both hardens the horn and kills the infection, but care must be taken not to breathe the vapour.

WINDGALLS

Windgalls are fluid-filled swellings just above the fetlock joints behind the cannon bone. Usually more than one leg is affected. The swelling is not painful or warm, and it does not cause lameness. It is worse when the horse rests in the stable than when it has been exercising. A windgall is basically a stretched portion of part of the fetlock joint capsule, so the fluid inside is joint fluid.

Action

Although windgalls can become very large in some horses, no action is really necessary because they are just a blemish. **Pressure bandaging may reduce the size of the swelling.** Removal of the fluid, and the injection of some cortisone may give a temporary improvement.

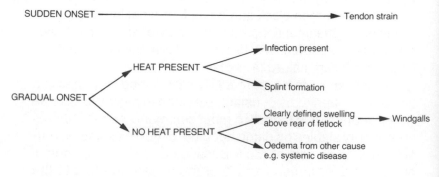

Fig 9 Causes of swelling behind the cannon bone

6 The Nervous System

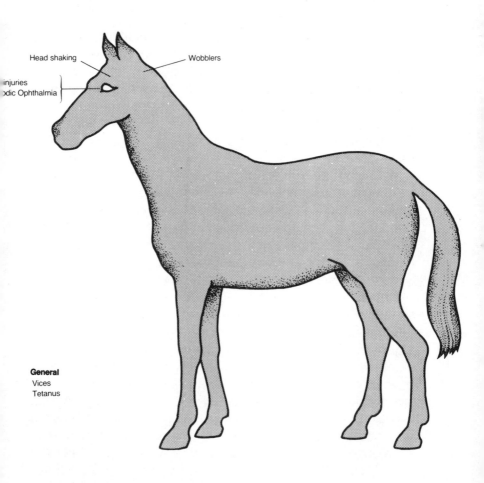

Head shaking

Wobblers

injuries
dic Ophthalmia

General
Vices
Tetanus

Although we speak of the nervous system, there are actually two separate systems. There is the system we normally think of, which controls conscious movements, and there is also a system which controls unconscious activities, such as heart rate. This is called the sympathetic system. Both are ultimately under the control of the central nervous system, which consists of the brain and spinal cord.

The nervous system operates in distinct physical halves on the left and right sides of the body. So an injury which affects one part of the central nervous system is more likely to affect parts of the same side of the body than parts of the other side. In the brain all these impulses are co-ordinated into one whole. A practical effect of this is that if you get a horse used to you doing something to one side of its body, such as grooming a nervous young horse, when you move over and try to groom the other side, the horse will react just as much as it did to your initial attempts, ie it will not carry across the information that your actions have not caused any pain and can safely be ignored.

Whilst on the subject of learning, it might be worthwhile pointing out that the horse is not a moral creature. It cannot make a distinction between the speed with which it learns good lessons and the speed with which it learns bad habits. So if you let a horse get away with some undesirable behaviour whilst training it do so something, you will teach it that undesirable behaviour just as firmly as your proper lesson.

One way in which we are only too aware of the nervous system is because it is responsible for the sensation of pain. There is an in-built reflex which makes a horse kick out when any part of its leg is hurt, for example. Domestication may blunt that reflex, but it is still basically there. The body does have its own mechanism for coping with pain. It produces its own painkillers in circumstances where survival may be helped if it cannot feel the pain. So if a galloping horse injures itself, it may secrete sufficient quantities of a natural morphine-like substance, called endorphin, to deaden the pain until the panic is over. When we put a twitch on a horse, this also stimulates the release of endorphins and so helps to deaden pain.

In addition to carrying impulses back to the central nervous system, nerves also carry the impulses out to muscles which tell them when to contract. If no such impulses pass along the relevant nerve, perhaps because it has been injured, then the muscle will be floppy and will not contract at all. It is then said to be paralysed. A paralysed muscle does not have anything wrong with it; it is in the nervous system that the fault lies. So if we stimulate the muscle artificially, the muscle will contract. Faradism is sometimes used to stimulate artificially such paralysed muscles in order to prevent them wasting away from disuse while an injured nerve heals itself.

Nerve injuries heal very slowly, but full return to normal function may occur. If we cut right through the nerve which receives sensations from the foot, in order to stop a horse with a chronic problem such as navicular disease staying lame, then over the course of two to three years most of the nerves will heal, and the sensation will return to the foot. If a nerve is damaged by constant pressure, and that pressure remains, such as occurs in the wobbler syndrome, then the nerve will never heal.

EYE INJURIES

The horse suffers relatively few eye injuries. The reason for this can readily be appreciated by anyone who has tried to hold open a horse's eye. The muscles around the eye react very quickly and strongly to any threat, closing the eye firmly. From time to time infections do become established in the eye, causing a discharge which may be clear or pussy and causing the pink membranes to become inflamed. The other common problem is the presence of a foreign body in the eye. As I have mentioned, it can be very difficult to detect such a foreign body without the use of local anaesthetics to prevent the horse closing its eyelids. When oats are being fed, occasionally an oat husk will get into the eye and become so adherent to the front surface, or cornea, that it is almost invisible to the naked eye but still causes intense irritation.

Action
If a horse is rubbing its eye or has an obvious discharge, first **clean the eye as much as possible using water, which has been boiled and allowed to cool down, and some cotton wool.** Use plenty of water, in order to wash the eye thoroughly. If that does not solve the problem, seek veterinary assistance as eyes are too sensitive to risk with home-made medication.

GRASS SICKNESS

Grass sickness is a disease of the nervous system, although the symptoms often primarily draw attention to the digestive tract. In its chronic form the first thing which the owner notices is a loss of condition which defies any efforts to feed the horse up. Gradually muscle-twitching develops over the body, especially the neck and shoulders. The horse may then be unwilling to swallow, first food and then water. By this stage the horse is standing in a dejected state, often with its head hanging over its manger, obviously in great pain. A green discharge may develop from its nostrils. Eventually the horse will die. Such a chronic form of the disease may take weeks or months from start to end. In other cases the course may be much more rapid, and in acute cases grass sickness can be fatal within 2-3 days.

The underlying problem is a nervous one. The ganglia, or control centres, of the nerves affecting the alimentary tract degenerate, causing paralysis of the parts supplied by those nerves. So on post-mortem examination we find that the whole alimentary tract has come to standstill. The green nasal discharge is actually stomach contents which, most unusually for the horse, can run back out of the stomach and up the oesophagus. Once one horse on the premises has succumbed to the disease you are quite likely to have other cases (though there may be months or years between them). Some sort of slow virus seems to be the likeliest culprit, but so far all attempts to find the cause have proved unsuccessful.

The disease was first diagnosed in Scotland, and has since slowly spread to the rest of Britain, especially on the east coast, and to parts of Europe. Surveys show that the disease almost always shows first in horses grazing on permanent pasture. Cases are commonest near the coast and during the spring time. Stress of some sort, such as moving the horse to new premises, is almost always involved in the initial case. Cisapride may keep the bowels moving and allow gradual recovery in some cases.

Action

Grass sickness is usually fatal. If cisapride does not produce bowel movement there is no real hope of recovery. For the horse's sake, all efforts must be concentrated on arriving as quickly as possible at an accurate diagnosis so that euthanasia can be carried out promptly if necessary. In most cases this involves eliminating all other causes of colic in the horse. It is claimed that a barium swallow test gives reliable diagnosis where the specialist equipment necessary to carry it out is available.

HEAD-SHAKING

Every horse shakes its head at some stage, and that does not cause any concern. When we use the term in the veterinary sense, we are referring to an uncontrollable shaking of the head, usually in an up and down direction, seen in horses which are being ridden. The movement can be so violent that the horse's head either hits the rider, or the rider is thrown off as he is caught unawares. The problem usually starts quite suddenly, often literally overnight. Once a horse is affected, however, it will almost always remain so for the rest of its life. The only consolation is that the symptoms do not occur during the cold months of winter.

Over 100 diseases have been implicated as the cause of head-shaking in one horse or another, including dental problems, ear mites and gutteral pouch problems. There still remain, however, a number of horses where the head-shaking has no apparent cause. Because the problem occurs in the summer, and is worst in warm humid conditions when flies abound, flies have been implicated in head-shaking. The problem may be worse, for example, around the edge of a field where the flies collect than it is in the centre of a windswept field. The mechanism by which the flies might be triggering off the problem has never been determined, although it is now thought that head-shaking is an allergic problem involving the linings of the nasal passages.

Action
The first step is to eliminate any obvious causes of the problem. So have the horse's teeth, ears and eyes examined. **Fitting a fly fringe around the forehead may reduce the problem,** as may avoiding riding in lanes or near hedgerows. If all else fails **it may only be possible to use the horse during the winter months.**

PERIODIC OPHTHALMIA

As its name implies this is an intermittent disease of the eye. It is also sometimes called moon blindness, because the cornea becomes opaque and white, and also because the symptoms may flare up and subside at approximately monthly intervals rather like the phases of the moon. The third, and most scientific, name for this disease is periodic uveitis. Again this emphasises that the condition comes and goes. It also stresses that it is the uvea, the part of the eye which forms the pupil and iris, which is most significantly involved. During an attack, one or both eyes may be affected. The pupil becomes constricted and this leads to problems with the fluids in the anterior chamber of the eye. The whole eye may be inflamed, so that the cornea becomes inflamed and opaque, there is a discharge from the eye and the eyelids may be swollen.

The cause of the condition is not completely clear. In some horses it has been associated with a Leptospirosis infection. In others it has been associated with an infestation with the *Onchocerca* parasite. In many cases no such links can be found. It would appear that the underlying problem is a hypersensitivity of some kind, hence the repeated upsurges of symptoms.

Action
Prompt veterinary attention is essential if the sight is not to be lost as a result of the problems following constriction of the pupil. Atropine drops are used to pull apart any adhesions and dilate the pupil again. Antibiotics and steroids may be injected actually into the conjunctival membranes around the eye. The prognosis is always guarded. The combination of sight loss and an acute reaction which affects the horse's whole demeanour, may make euthanasia necessary.

TETANUS

Tetanus is a bacterial disease, caused by a bacterium called *Clostridium tetani,* but the devastating symptoms are the result of a toxin released into the general circulation. The bacterium gains entry via a wound in the skin or an abrasion in the intestinal wall. Because the bacterium only multplies in low concentrations of oxygen, it is deep penetrating wounds which pose the greatest threat. The bacterium does not spread away from the site of entry, but it does release large amounts of toxin. The tetanus toxin affects nerves to cause spasm of the muscles they supply.

A horse with tetanus usually starts by developing a stiff gait. Muscles over the body may then start twitching uncontrollably. It is said to be diagnostic for tetanus that if you raise the horse's head up high, the third eyelid is pulled across the eyeball from the front corner of the eye. Affected horses over-react to stimuli such as noise or sudden movements. Eventually the horse cannot stand, and death occurs because the muscles of breathing are affected.

Action
All horses should be vaccinated against tetanus at least every two years. The vaccine is called tetanus toxoid, and two initial injections are needed to stimulate immunity. **Any horse which acquires even a small skin wound should have an immediate injection of tetanus antitoxin unless you are absolutely sure that it has been fully vaccinated.** As its name implies, the antitoxin neutralises the effect of the tetanus toxin. The use of antitoxin is not 100 per cent reliable, it is very like shutting the stable door after the horse has bolted. You will never know, for example, if tetanus bacteria have penetrated a wound in the bowel wall.

Not all horses which get tetanus die. Large doses of antibiotic and tetanus antitoxin may neutralise the infection, although it is often necessary to support the horse in slings for a considerable time if the muscles of the legs are affected.

VICES

A vice is a behavioural habit which may have harmful effects on the horse. Vices are not diseases as such, and so are not within the scope of a veterinary examination prior to purchase. They are sufficiently serious for the Conditions of Sale at most horse sales to allow the immediate return to the vendor of any horse found suffering from one of these stable vices following purchase. Crib-biting, wind-sucking and weaving are all recognised vices, to which some people would add box-walking.

Crib-biting is the act of the horse fastening its front incisor teeth on a fixed object, such as the top of the stable door, and bracing the muscles of its neck before letting go. This causes considerable damage to the woodwork of the stable, fencing etc. During the action, wood may be ground off the object and swallowed. The front teeth become abnormally worn, and this can make ageing the horse rather difficult. In many cases horses which crib-bite progress to being wind-suckers.

Wind-sucking consists of the horse fixing the muscles of its throat, usually but not always by crib-biting, and then swallowing air. This action is claimed to make some horses unthrifty because their stomachs are full of air rather than food. It has also been claimed that such horses are more prone to colic.

When a horse weaves, it stands still and transfers its weight from one front leg to another, moving its neck from side to side as it does so. Horses usually weave as they stand at a doorway. Box-walking is simply what its name implies: the horse just keeps on walking round and round its box. This is obviously a tiring and wasteful activity.

It is a feature of stable vices that they are contagious. Once one horse in a yard starts performing a particular activity, other horses in the yard will often follow suit. Vices appear to be a response to stress, which is why horses will often perform them when they move to a strange place. Once a horse has established a vice for more than a few days, it will often continue to do so for the rest of its life. Apparently vices stimulate the release of endorphins, natural morphine derivatives, into the horse's blood stream. They can therefore be considered as self-inflicted dope taking.

Action

Vices have traditionally been blamed on boredom. Accordingly, **the first step in their elimination is to relieve boredom** by more frequent exercise periods, distractions such as rubber tyres hanging from the ceiling of the box, and making sure that the horse can see as much as possible of any activity which is taking place in the yard.

Crib-biting, and wind-sucking when they are associated, may be prevented by strapping a specially shaped rigid yoke on top of the larynx, or voice box. As long as this is strapped in place firmly enough, it will prevent the horse fixing its larynx into the position needed to give it the satisfaction which is the reason behind its performing the vice. In severe cases, surgery is possible to remove a portion of the nerves and muscles responsible for the action.

WOBBLERS

A wobbler is a young horse which progressively loses the control of its hind limbs, until eventually it will become unable to stand. Although this is a rare condition, there is a significantly higher percentage in young Arabs. The condition can show itself at any time during the first two or three years of life. At first the horse only appears to have a sloppy action on its hind legs. Then its hind quarters start to sway during movement. The problem is more marked at the walk or when turning in a small circle. At the gallop the horse may have a 'bunny-hopping' action.

The problem is due to a degeneration in the spinal cord of the neck, often as a result of pressure from the bony spinal canal. Sometimes it is confirmed by X-rays. Pulling sideways on the horse's tail as it moves may almost pull an affected horse right over. The actual site of the problem in the neck can vary, although the symptoms will be the same.

Action
The condition is basically incurable. In the USA major surgery is sometimes performed to relieve the pressure on the spinal cord, but this has not been ethically well received in the UK. Euthanasia is usually performed as soon as a precise diagnosis has been made.

7 The Digestive System

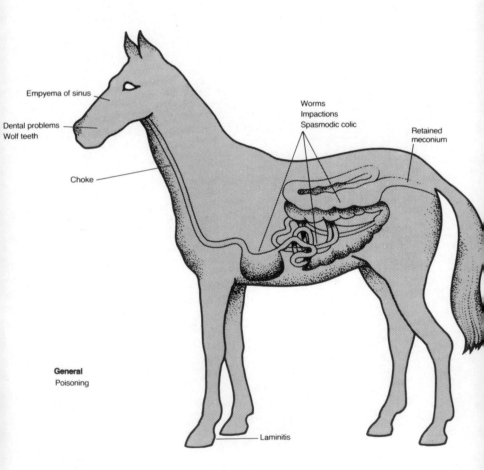

Empyema of sinus

Dental problems
Wolf teeth

Choke

Worms
Impactions
Spasmodic colic

Retained
meconium

General
Poisoning

Laminitis

The feeding of a horse is outside the scope of a book such as this, except when poor management leads to a physical disturbance, such as choke. Even when good quality food is fed at regular intervals, the horse can still develop major malfunctions of its digestive tract because it is such a complex system. Good clean water is just as essential to the horse as food, in fact more so in the short term because a horse which is in good bodily condition will usually die from dehydration before it does from starvation.

In nature the horse grazes, so little chewing is needed from the molar, or cheek, teeth before the food is swallowed into the oesophagus. During the chewing, however, saliva is mixed with the food. Food reaches the stomach in a more or less continuous dribble, and so the horse's stomach is only small because it never has a large quantities to deal with at any one time. At the entrance to the stomach is quite a tight sphincter, which prevents the horse from vomiting except in extraordinary circumstances. Digestion takes place in the stomach and the small and large intestines. In the case of the latter, the digestion is carried out by millions of bacteria which trade the safety of living inside the horse's large colon for the benefit which the horse obtains by absorbing the simple foodstuffs they manufacture from the fibrous, cellulose part of its diet.

Non-digested material, plus certain waste products from the body, are excreted as faeces, or dung. This is normally formed into balls, but can be softer or even liquid in certain disease states. Of course, during grazing all sorts of bacteria are taken into the digestive tract. The fact that relatively few of these manage to establish themselves and cause infection is due to a very efficient defence mechanism. The stomach contents are highly acidic, and this acidity kills off most types of bacteria. Further down the digestive tract, the sheer weight of numbers of established 'friendly' bacteria will often overwhelm any living bacteria which still survive.

CHOKE

A choked horse is not usually one with something stuck in its mouth or throat; such obstructions can be coughed free. The term 'choked' is taken to mean a horse with an oesophageal obstruction. This may be caused by a variety of things. It may be a solid object which the horse swallows by mistake but which is too large to pass down the oesophagus, or gullet. Carrots and potatoes are the commonest causes of choke in this category. On the other hand, the problem may be caused by something which swells up as it passes down the oesophagus until it can go no further. This occurs because whatever a horse swallows is accompanied by copious amounts of saliva, and the material absorbs this liquid and increases in size accordingly. Dried sugar beet pulp, in various forms, is the commonest cause of choke in this category.

A choked horse is obviously distressed. It stands with its head hanging low, but may be apprehensive of any attempt to investigate the problem. The most obvious symptom is usually the fact that saliva is drooling from the mouth because it cannot pass down the oesophagus but is being produced in increased amounts. The horse may stand over its water bucket or manger, but appears unable to swallow even liquid. The presence of the saliva in the pharynx at the back of the mouth may make breathing very noisy, falsely giving the impression that the problem is a respiratory one. If the choke is not relieved, the horse may indeed suck saliva down its trachea into its lungs.

Action

Prompt veterinary attention is needed. The horse should be kept as quiet as possible, with its head down to allow the saliva to drain forward and so reduce the risk of it going down into the lungs. All food and water should be removed. If it is obvious that there is a solid object stuck in the oesophagus, and this can be felt because the oesophagus only has a thin wall, then gentle massage of the area may help the horse to move the offending object on.

An injection of a sedative and/or mild muscle relaxant may allow the wall of the oesophagus to relax enough to free the obstruction. Small solid obstructions may be pushed on down the oesophagus, but this does carry some risk of tearing the oesophageal wall and so is not attempted on larger foreign bodies. Food material like carrots will, in time, be eaten away by the digestive enzymes of the saliva, although this requires careful 24-hour nursing in the intervening period. Sugar beet pulp is removed by using a stomach tube to alternately pump in a small amount of water and then suck out the mixture of beet pulp and water which is formed. It can be a slow and laborious process.

Most cases of choke can be prevented by attention to detail in feeding. Large, solid material such as carrots should either be left whole, so that the horse appreciates that it must chew them fully, or cut so small that they cannot cause a problem. **Sugar beet pulp must always be soaked so thoroughly that it is not possible for it to absorb any more liquid. This means at least 12 hours soaking, and checking that there is still excess liquid present before feeding.** If there is no excess liquid present, you do not know whether the wet-looking mass has absorbed all the water you added but can still absorb more. Special care must be taken to ensure that there is no way that a horse can obtain access to either the soaking sugar beet pulp, or the stored, dry material. If you delegate the task of feeding the horse to anyone else, be sure that they are aware of these dangers. Many cases of choke with sugar beet pulp arise from the ignorance of someone other than the owner. Because of this, some people have got the idea that sugar beet pulp is a dangerous food for horses. It is not dangerous in itself, only when people are careless or try to cut corners by reducing the soaking time. Used properly it is a very valuable feedstuff.

DENTAL PROBLEMS

The structure of the horse's molar, or cheek, teeth, with a sloping grinding surface means that there is an in-built tendency to form sharp edges on the teeth. These sharp points come to damage the inside of the cheeks and the tongue, causing considerable discomfort during feeding. So a horse with sharp molars tends to eat less, especially concentrates which need more chewing. When the horse is being ridden, the bridle presses the skin of the cheeks against the sharp points on the outside of the upper molars and as a result the horse does not respond to the bit as well as it might otherwise do. Obviously the degree to which the owner notices these problems depends on careful observation and knowledge of the horse's past performance. I should point out that horses of all ages can develop molar points: they are not the sole prerogative of old horses.

Fig 10 Ageing the horse by dentition
Although widely used, it has been shown that these changes can be very misleading, especially when ageing horses over 5 years old.

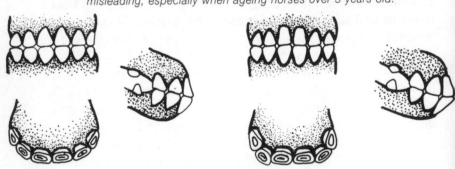

2 years (all milk teeth)   3 years (two central permanent teeth)

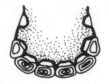

4 years (four
permanent teeth)

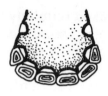

5 years (all six permanent teeth present)

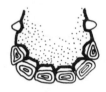

7 years

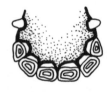

10 years (Galvayne's groove appears in upper corner incisor tooth)

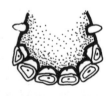

15 years

30 years

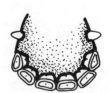

Action

All horses should have their teeth checked regularly (ie at least once a year) for sharp points. You can obtain some idea of the existence or otherwise of a problem by grasping hold of your horse's tongue with one hand, holding it out of one side of its mouth so that it is less likely to close its mouth completely, and feeling the teeth of the other side with your other hand. You will not, however, be able to feel the back molars, nor any points on the inside of the bottom teeth, so this method cannot be relied upon. For a thorough examination a mouth gag is necessary. This holds the horse's jaws firmly and safely open so that the teeth can be examined at leisure. Any sharp points or hooks can then be filed off with a tooth rasp. The process does not hurt the horse at all.

EMPYEMA OF A FRONTAL SINUS

Empyema, or pus in a sinus, is almost always due to an infection gaining entry into one of the sinuses of the head or face via one of the molar teeth. The roots of some of these teeth extend into the sinuses, and the infection either travels around the surface of the tooth itself or up a damaged root canal.

The symptoms are a swelling of the bone over the sinus, and a pussy nasal discharge down one of the nostrils. It is the fact that the discharge is only from one nostril, and always the same one, which gives rise to suspicion that it originates from a sinus rather than the respiratory tract. X-rays will show both the damaged tooth root, and possibly also the level of the pus in the cavity of the sinus.

Action

The only way to treat this problem is to remove the affected tooth under general anaesthesia. The focus of the infection is thus removed, and with repeated washing out of the sinus with water (via the hole made in the skull to push out the tooth) coupled with antibiotic therapy, the infection is overcome. Antibiotic therapy without removal of the tooth will never bring about a permanent cure.

IMPACTIONS

An impaction is a blockage, or stoppage, of some part of the alimentary tract. Impactions can arise from a number of causes. Perhaps the commonest is a failure of the horse to digest fibrous food properly in the colon. Material then accumulates at the pelvic flexure of the large colon, where the colon decreases in diameter by 50 per cent and bends through 180°. Other causes of an impaction include tapeworms in adult horses and large numbers of ascarid worms in young horses. Worm damage to large sections of the intestines can disrupt normal bowel movements and allow an impaction to form. Grazing of poor quality pasture can lead to the horse taking in large amounts of soil and silt which can cause an impaction of the caecum.

A horse with an impaction is first and foremost a miserable horse. It may just stand there, looking very dejected, but more often it will lie down on its side. It may lie so still that you can hardly see it breathing, and it will be very reluctant to get up on its feet. At first it will continue to pass faeces, but as all the faeces behind the impaction are expelled no more droppings will appear. A rectal examination may enable the veterinary surgeon to feel the actual impaction, and to remove some of the remaining faeces. An affected horse eats little. If the impaction is not relieved, the horse gets more and more toxic. Its mucous membranes around the eyes, for example, may become very red and congested. Eventually the horse will die.

Action
Undoubtedly some impactions are very temporary. The intestinal contents are only held up temporarily, and then

move on again. So **if you have a mild suspicion that a horse has an impaction, you should give it a good warm bran mash and wait for an hour to see if it improves. If it does not do so, veterinary help should be called.** The usual treatment is to give quite large volumes of purgatives such as liquid paraffin via a stomach tube. You should not attempt to give purgatives yourself by drenching. The risk of the liquid going down the horse's trachea into its lungs rather than down its oesophagus far outweighs any slight financial gain from possibly saving a vet's bill. Treatment may need to be repeated for several days until the impaction is softened enough to move it on. During this time painkillers may be given, but you should be warned that they are often ineffective against this form of pain. The drug flunixen may be effective, but then there is the risk that it may hide the fact that the horse's condition is really getting worse rather than better. In severe cases surgery may be needed to remove the impacted material.

The best way to avoid impactions is to avoid sudden changes in diet. The bacteria in the horse's colon will adjust to provide the most efficient digestion of the food mix they are receiving, but they take several days to do so. A sudden change, such as starting to stable the horse or changing from one type of hay to another, provides enough disruption for digestion to come to a standstill.

LAMINITIS

I have included laminitis as a digestive problem rather than a problem associated with movement in order to emphasise that it has its origins in what the horse eats. Acute laminitis is triggered off by too much carbohydrate in the stomach, ie over-eating. During the stomach's attempt to cope with this overload, increased levels of histamine are produced. This affects various parts of the body to some extent or other, but its most dramatic effect is on the feet. The histamine cuts down blood flow through the blood vessels of the sensitive laminae between the hoof and the pedal bone. Much of the blood which is pumped down the arteries of the leg then bypasses around the coronet without going into the foot at all. The blood which pools in the foot itself does not supply enough oxygen, and tissues start to degenerate. In particular, the sensitive laminae degenerate and no longer hold the pedal bone against the front wall of the hoof. This may allow the bone to rotate until the tip of the bone is pressing downwards through the sole of the hoof.

Laminitis is a lameness of all four feet, and is almost unique in this respect. That is not to say that all four feet will be affected to the same degree. The front feet always bear more weight than the back feet, so they will always show more pain. The horse walks with very short strides, giving a pottery gait. As it does not know which foot to put most weight on, it may walk 'like a cat on a hot tin roof'. In acute cases, the horse may not be willing to walk at all, just standing with its weight on its heels, rocking backwards and forwards slightly. Examining

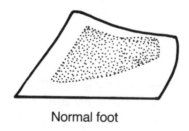

Normal foot

granulation tissue
filling space left by rotation

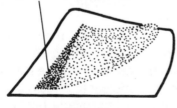

Laminitic foot

Fig 11 Rotation of the pedal bone in laminitis

the feet can be difficult because the horse is unable to bear enough extra weight on the other three feet to enable it to lift one foot up. Sometimes the feet are warm to the touch, but this is not always the case. The warmth is not due to increased blood flow through the foot, as used to be thought. It is due to the blood flowing more slowly and thus having more time to pass on its heat, in the same way that the longer you hold your hand on a radiator, the hotter the radiator feels. Because of the disruption of blood flow at the end of the system, a strong pulse may be felt as the main artery and vein pass down the posterior third of the postern.

Chronic changes may follow laminitis. I have already mentioned that the point of the pedal bone can cause pressure on the sole, and may penetrate it. X-rays are often vital to check whether the pedal bone has started to rotate or not. The sensitive laminae may be so disrupted that the hoof is no longer attached to the pedal bone at all, and literally drops off. More commonly, attacks of laminitis leave the horn of the hoof ringed where the nutrition of the horn has been disrupted.

Action

In mild attacks of laminitis, the administration of pain-killers such as phenylbutazone and acetylpromazine to help restore normal blood pressure may be all that is required to return blood flow in the foot to normal. The diet should be drastically reduced in nutritional value, and some mashes given to speed up the passage of the culprit carbohydrate through the bowels. The horse should be box rested.

In many cases overgrown feet play a major role in both impeding circulation and increasing the forces pulling the hoof wall away from the bone. So **have the feet trimmed as soon as possible.** In some cases it may take major resection of the front wall of the hoof to restore normal hoof shape and alter the angle of the foot enough to compensate for any pedal bone rotation. Fitting a heart bar shoe will give extra support to the pedal bone via the frog.

It is doubtful whether applying cold to the warm feet of a horse with laminitis does any good, but **hosing and standing in fast flowing water may have a slight advantageous effect on the circulation.** There is some evidence that drugs such as isoxsuprine and clenbuterol increase the blood flow through the actual foot, and so relieve the condition.

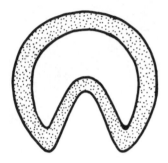

Fig 12 Heart bar shoe for laminitis

POISONING

It is obviously outside the scope of a book of this sort to describe the symptoms of every kind of poisoning which might affect a horse. There are two common poisonous plants which every horse owner should be aware of. Although the yew tree is not a very common tree, it retains its importance because it is so toxic. The symptom of yew tree poisoning is death. Horses which eat even a small amount of the leaves die suddenly, possibly still with some of the leaves in their mouth. There is therefore no treatment, and no action which owners can take except to ensure that their horse never gains access to any part of a yew tree.

Ragwort poisoning, on the other hand, is often a very slow process, because the toxic alkaloid involved is a cumulative poison. An affected horse may lose weight over weeks or months. Alternatively if a large quantity of ragwort is eaten during a short time, the horse may become acutely ill. It will

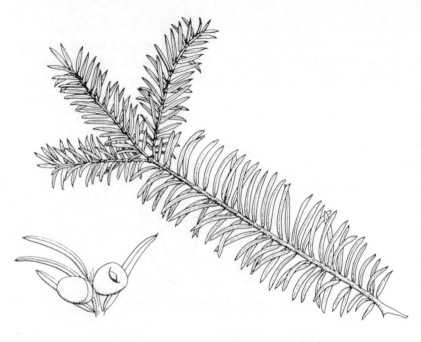

Fig 13 Yew (drawing by Rosemary Wise)

then stagger around, as if it was sleepy and unaware of its surroundings. At this time it can pose a real threat to any person near to it who might be crushed. Eventually the horse goes into a coma and dies.

Action

All parts of the ragwort plant are poisonous. The plant is even poisonous in the dried state in hay. You should not rely on the supposed bitter taste of the plant to prevent your horse eating ragwort. Once a horse gets a taste for it (perhaps because it is the greenest plant in the field at a particular time of year) it will seek the plant out. Frequent spraying can kill the plants, although care must be taken not to graze the field until all the dead plants have rotted away. **Pulling the plants up by hand, roots and all, remains the most effective way of controlling ragwort on small paddocks. Fields containing ragwort should never be used for hay.**

120

There is little that can be done for clinically affected horses, especially if blood samples show that considerable liver damage has already occurred. Intravenous infusions of glucose solution may help in mild cases, but often euthanasia is the only humane course of action.

Fig 14 Ragwort

RETAINED MECONIUM

Retained meconium is a condition of the very young foal, during the first two or three days of life. Meconium is the faeces which the foal forms as it grows in the mare's uterus. It is bright orange or blackish green in colour, and there may be 12-18in in length of this material. If the foal fails to push the meconium out soon after birth, it becomes impacted and hard. The foal then becomes toxic and stops suckling the mare. It may have a raised temperature. Usually the foal will stand and strain as it tries unsuccessfully to pass the meconium. Without treatment, it may die. Colt foals are more prone to retention of their meconium than fillies, due to the anatomy of their pelvis.

Action
All foals should be watched closely until they have passed all their meconium and are passing normal faeces. Ensuring that a foal sucks a normal amount of the mare's colostrum within the first 6-8 hours of its life will help because this has a laxative effect. **Any foal which stops suckling within the first two or three days of life should be examined** for such an impaction. Foals may pass some of the meconium and appear to be alright, but then become impacted on the last portion of the material. Breeders may administer a human micro-enema into the foal's rectum in an attempt to get things moving. If this does not work within an hour, then veterinary assistance should be sought because time runs out quickly in newborn animals.

SPASMODIC COLIC

Colic is abdominal pain. It may become apparent in a number of ways. The horse may stand looking around at its flank. It may kick at its flank. Often affected horses will repeatedly lie down and roll. If the pain is very great they may literally throw themselves to the ground, with no respect for any thing or person who may be in the way. Horses with colic may sweat profusely in patches over their body. In spasmodic colic the horse is in pain for perhaps 30-60 minutes, but the pain then appears to subside, only to return after a short period.

Colic can be triggered off by a variety of causes. Horse owners appear convinced that every case of acute colic pain is caused by a twisted gut. This is not the case, in fact an actual twist in the intestines is rather rare. Most spasmodic colics are due to disruption of the normal automatic bowel movements. Changes in diet or routine, even something which upsets the horse, can trigger it off. American surveys blame up to 80 per cent of colic on worm problems. Migrating worm larvae damage the lining of the blood vessels which supply sections of the intestines. Necrosis, or death, of the intestinal wall tissues causes pain, and the absence of food movement through the affected section also causes pain.

Perhaps the most acute pain is caused by displacement of a section of the intestines from its normal position in the abdomen. Whole loops of intestine can become trapped in the mesentery, or membranes, which are supporting other sections. In such a case the pain becomes continuous and very acute. There is an old wives' tale that if you allow a horse with colic to roll, it will cause a twist in the bowels and so change an ordinary problem into a very serious, and potentially fatal, one. This is not the case; there is no evidence that a sudden deterioration in the horse's condition is due to a twist suddenly occurring. All the evidence shows that the physical problem has been there from the start. It is the increasing effects of shock which cause the sudden deterioration in the horse's condition.

Action

First of all, horse owners should know how to distinguish when a case of colic is extremely serious and potentially fatal. This is relatively easy to do. **If the horse has a high temperature, above 103°F (39.4°C), then the pain is serious. If the horse's pulse is above 60 per minute, it is serious, especially if**

the pulse is at all irregular. Finally, and most significantly, if the horse has a capillary refill time of more than 4 seconds, then it is very serious. You detect this by pressing with your thumb on the pink membranes of the horse's gums. When you remove your thumb, the gum looks pale and white. The capillary refill time is the time it takes for the normal pink colour to return to the membranes. **If you get a positive reaction to these tests, contact your veterinary surgeon at once,** telling him what you have found so that he knows the exact situation.

In less dramatic situations, many horse owners respond to colic by walking the horse around for an hour or so and hoping that it will improve. This is a pointless activity which will only tire the horse just at a time when it may need all its strength. As I have described, there is no danger that a horse will make the colic worse by rolling, so **there is no need to walk the horse** in an attempt to stop it doing so. All too often the horse then throws itself to the ground outside and rolls anyway, but in a much more dangerous environment than in its stable. The only danger from rolling is that the horse may be so violent that it poses a real danger of breaking a limb etc. by its actions, and no amount of walking will control that kind of pain.

Although there are proprietary colic drinks sold by saddlers, I consider them extremely dangerous. Pouring fluid down a

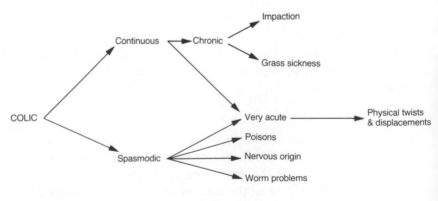

Fig 15 Types of colic

horse's mouth gives you only a little better than a 50/50 chance of its going down the oesophagus rather than the traachea. This especially so in a frightened horse in pain from colic. In any case, the quantity of liquid and medicaments contained in such drinks is insignificant for a gastro-intestinal tract the size of that in the horse. When veterinary surgeons give fluids by stomach tube to horses with colic they will administer several litres at a time, not tens or hundreds of millilitres.

Home treatment of colic largely consists of reassurance for the apprehensive horse. Make sure that there is a thick, dry bed. Try and persuade the horse to take a warm bran mash. Above all, if mild pain persists for more than 30 minutes, or if it returns after a period of relief, call your veterinary surgeon. In cases of acute pain, call the veterinary surgeon immediately.

We now have a number of very effective painkilling drugs which can control the pain in colic. In most cases, this is sufficient to allow the resumption of normal bowel contractions and relaxations. There is a slight danger that we are now able to make horses with serious physical displacements and twists appear to be 'cured' after treatment. By the time the drug wears off (which may take as long as 8-12 hours) and we find out that the horse is not cured, the condition may have deteriorated considerably. Increasingly surgery is being used to investigate and correct such serious types of colic. Surgery stands the best chance of being successful if it is carried out early rather than late. The success rate at the specialist clinics carrying out such surgery can be as high as 50-70 per cent of cases, so many horses which would previously have died in agony are now being saved.

Effective routine worm control is the best preventive measure that can be taken against colic, given that up to 80 per cent of colics are associated in some way with worm infestations. **Regular feeding of unchanging rations will also help, especially if the horse's teeth are regularly rasped to ensure that the food is properly chewed.**

WORMS

There are a number of stomach and intestinal worms which can infest the horse. They have different lifestyles, affect the horse in different ways, and are killed by different drugs. Considerable thought must therefore be given to drawing up a preventive programme which will ensure that your horse remains free from such parasites.

Ascarids are worms which affect young horses. This is because, almost uniquely for worms, adult horses develop an effective resistance to the worms. Unfortunately no-one has yet managed to convert this natural situation to the production of a commercial vaccine against ascarids. The main member of the family to cause problems is *Parascaris equorum*. The adult worm is quite large, and if present in reasonable numbers can physically block the lumen of the foal's intestines. This is a point to watch after treating an ascarid infection because you may see signs of colic as the dying worms cause a temporary obstruction. The adult worms release eggs which pass out onto the pasture with the horse's droppings. In the case of ascarids, the eggs have a very thick coat, and so can survive on the pasture for a year or more. This is how the parasite survives from one foal crop to another despite the resistance which horses build up to it. A horse takes in hatched worm larvae with the grass it is feeding on. These larvae do not, however, immediately mature to adult worms. First they migrate through the body. In the case of ascarids they migrate through the liver and lungs before returning to the stomach and intestines as adult worms which can lay more eggs. The migration through the lungs can cause symptoms of respiratory disease, which are known as 'summer cold'. The young horse may have a raised temperature, and has a nasal discharge. Its breathing rate is increased.

The other worm which poses a particular threat to young horses is *Strongyloides westerii*. In this case it is the very short life cycle, from laying eggs to the development of adult worms again, which enables large numbers of the worm to accumulate even in young horses.

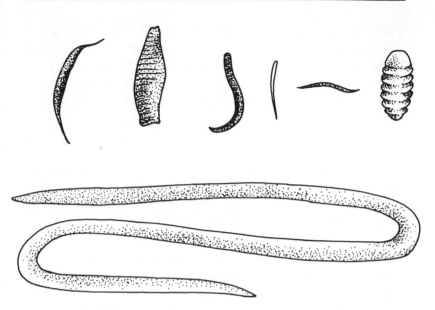

Fig 16 Common worms of the horse. Left to right: oxyuris, tapeworm, strongylus edentatus, two examples of strongylus vulgaris, bot larva. Below: parascoris equorum

A major worm threat to adult horses is *Strongylus vulgaris*, one of the so-called 'large red worms'. With this worm it is not the damage to the intestinal wall which poses the threat, nor is it the amount of blood sucked by the adult worm (which gives it the red colour). The major threat is not from the nutrients taken by the worm rather than the horse. Rather, it is the physical damage caused during the migration of immature larvae. These burrow into the small arteries in the intestinal wall, and literally swim against the blood flow until they reach a point where the blood vessels radiate out to supply a loop of intestine, rather like the hub of a bicycle wheel. The larvae remain here for about four months, during which time they cause damage to the blood vessel wall which may cause the lumen of the blood vessel to become partially or completely blocked by a blood clot, or thrombus. When this maturing period is over the larvae migrate back to the intestinal wall, and through into its lumen again as adult worms.

127

You will now appreciate why this worm can cause colic. The reduced blood supply to a loop of bowel causes pain because of anoxia, or lack of oxygen. The small strongyles are causing an increasing number of problems. One reason for this is their high incidence of resistance to benzimidazole wormers. The worms cause local damage in the bowel wall, especially if large numbers of larvae emerge into the bowel at the same time.

I do not propose to discuss in detail all the different species of worm which can infest the horse, but there are two other cases which perhaps should be mentioned. *Oxyuris equi*, or the pin worm, does not affect the horse's body as such, but because the adult worms live just inside the rectum, and may crawl out onto the skin around the rectum, they can cause irritation. A horse which rubs its tail area does not always have sweet itch, it may have a pin worm infestation. The other oddity is the horse bot, *Gastrophilus*. This is not a worm at all, but a fly. The fly lays its eggs on the horse's skin, especially the legs. These cream-coloured eggs can be readily seen attached to the hairs during the summer months. When the eggs hatch, the larvae penetrate into the skin and migrate to the horse's stomach, where they form the bot. Very large numbers of bots can cause ulceration of the stomach wall. In the following spring, the life cycle continues to the adult fly. So bots are only an internal problem during the winter months, although the adult flies may cause some annoyance as they lay their eggs.

Action

It is not practicable to devise separate control programmes for each parasite. You have to strike a balance between what you can afford in the way of drugs and time, and what is needed to eliminate the degree of challenge on your pasture. Horses which are stabled 24 hours a day, 365 days a year will not pick up any new worms. Once their existing worm burdens have been killed off, no further measures will be necessary. Very few horses are not put out to grass at some time, however.

As grazing is the source of all worm infestations, control measures should start with the paddocks. If a field has not been grazed by horses for at least two years, it will have only a negligible worm burden. There are no chemicals which can be spread over a pasture to kill off worm eggs. Harrowing will break up the balls of faeces, exposing the eggs to drying, which will kill them. **Removing the faeces** by hand is a very effective way of controlling worms if you have sufficient labour available for the area of grazing. Such removal must be carried out every other day if it is to be effective. If you leave a longer period between collections, the worm larvae will have hatched and moved out of the faeces by the time you remove them.

Most worm larvae climb up the stalks of the grass after hatching, in order to ensure that even if only a little of the grass is eaten, they will be included. So **topping,** or removing the top of the grass to leave grass of a uniform length, **will reduce the numbers of larvae sitting waiting to be eaten.** The larvae are still left on the paddock though. **Grazing with other species of animals, such as sheep and cattle, will** not only **help** the pasture by eating the areas which the horses have left, but will actually kill the larvae as they pass through the animals' stomachs.

Many owners place all their reliance for worm control on the use of anthelmintics, or anti-worm drugs. It is important to realise that the aim of anthelmintics is not to kill off the adult worms which happen to be present on the day of dosing. They will do that, but in many cases it is not the adult worms which cause the most serious problems. **The main aim of anthelmintic dosing is to reduce the number of eggs passed out onto the pasture, and so reduce the future risk of infection.** When deciding how often you need to administer a particular drug to your horse, the period should be set so that the next dose is given before enough new adult worms have matured to be releasing significant numbers of eggs in the faeces. With most wormers this will mean **dosing approximately every 6 to 8 weeks.** With a drug like ivermectin which, in addition to adults, kills immature worm larvae as they migrate through the body, then the period will be slightly longer. Worming just twice a year, or worming merely during the summer grazing months, will have very little effect on the worm challenge. In the case of the latter, you must remember that immature *Strongylus vulgaris* larvae will continue to mature into adults for up to six months after the horse last grazes infected pasture, and most drugs have no effect on these larvae until they become adults.

The remaining question is 'which anthelmintic should you use?' The number of choices is not as great as you might think. More than half of the available drugs belong to the same chemical family. They can be recognised by the fact that their chemical names all end in -ndazole. Although these drugs have individual advantages and disadvantages, worms which become resistant to one member of the family usually also become resistant to the other members. So there is no point in changing from one member of the group to another. **If you use a drug which has never had any resistance (and both pyrantel and ivermectin fall into this category) then there is no need ever to change wormers to avoid resistance.** You might want to change for other reasons. For instance, **pyrantel at a double dose kills tapeworms** but ivermectin does not, whereas **ivermectin kills immature larvae** whereas pyrantel does not. But that is a different matter. In any case, alternating wormers is never a good idea. It is really not much better than worming at half the normal frequency with each drug. If you are worried about resistance, it is probably better to use one drug for a number of wormings and then change. There is then a good chance that by the time you return to the original drug any resistance acquired will have been lost.

Anthelmintics can be administered in three ways. Giving them in food is easy, but it is difficult to ensure that a full dose is consumed within a short time. Eating it over the course of a day may mean that effective concentrations are never reached. There is also the problem of other horses sharing the food if the horse is out at grass. Giving the anthelmintic as a paste, using a plastic syringe and squirting it into the horse's tongue, is safe and reliable. It usually costs more because of the cost of the syringe. In some parts of the world owners are apparently unable to squirt a syringe into their horse's mouth, and they have to pay their veterinary surgeon to pass a stomach tube down their horse's oesophagus and pump in a liquid containing the anthelmintic.

Because you do not see actual worms in your horse's faeces, there is an uncertainty as to whether your control programme is working or not. There are ways of checking this. A faeces sample can be examined under a microscope, and the number of worm eggs present counted. This worm count gives a rough (but only rough) assessment of how many adult worms are present. In the case of *Strongylus vulgaris*, for

Selecting a Wormer			
WORMER	EXTRA ACTIVITY	PASTE AVAILABLE	RESISTANCE
DICHLORVOS	also treats bots	−	
FEBANTEL		−	
HALOXON	some bot activity	*	
OXIBENDAZOLE		*	
MEBENDAZOLE		*	
THIABENDAZOLE	needs double dose for ascarids	*	
FENBENDAZOLE	needs higher dose for lungworm & worm larvae	*	
OXFENDAZOLE	some worm larvae activity	*	
IVERMECTIN	active lungworm & worm larvae	*	No resistance reported despite years of use
METRIPHONATE	only bots, ascarids & oxyuris	*	
PYRANTEL	active tapeworms at double dose	*	No resistance reported despite years of use

example, you will not get a reading until about six months after the worms enter the horse's body. A blood sample can give information about the presence of worms, whether adult or immature, by looking at the proteins which are associated with the horse's immune response to the worms. This does not give an indication of numbers, but it does give an earlier result.

WOLF TEETH

Wolf teeth are small pre-molar teeth which are present on some, but not all, horses. They are commonest in the upper jaw and occur immediately adjacent to the first normal molar tooth. They should not be confused with the tushes, or canine teeth, which occur in male horses midway between the incisor teeth and the molars. Wolf teeth are only embedded in the gums, and do not have a root into the jaw. Consequently they can be 'rocked' by pressure from the bit. Horses vary in the amount of resentment they may or may not show to this.

Action
If the horse is going to be asked to carry out work which requires very precise responses to the bit, such as dressage, or if a horse with wolf teeth shows any resentment of the bit at all, then the wolf teeth should be removed. This is a relatively simply procedure which is carried out in the conscious horse, and causes surprisingly little pain.

8 The Urinary And Reproductive System

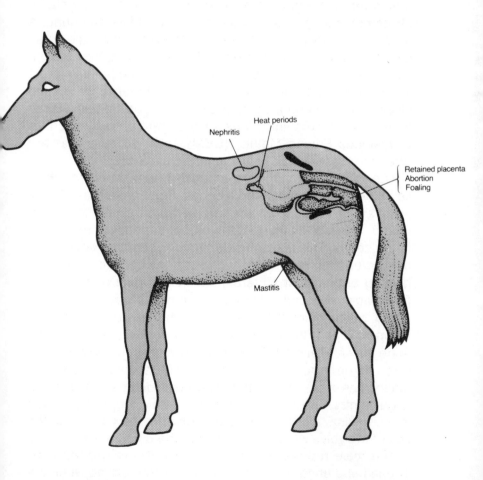

Nephritis

Heat periods

Retained placenta
Abortion
Foaling

Mastitis

It is customary to discuss the urinary system and the reproductive system together for the simple reason that in both sexes they share a common outlet. Problems with the urinary system are relatively rare in horses, possibly because few horses live to be really old in the way that people do; their lives are ended when they lose their athletic abilities.

The urinary system starts with the two kidneys, where the urine is produced by filtering water and certain undesirable substances out of the blood stream. A small tube, the ureter, drains the urine into the bladder, which has the capacity to stretch to many times its 'normal' size as it fills with urine. A single tube, the urethra, drains the bladder. In the male horse it leads to the penis, whereas in the mare it empties into the vagina just behind the lips of the vulva. At the point where it joins the vagina, there is a small protuberance called the clitoris. The importance of this is that if swabs are being taken to try and culture infections of the genital tract, such as Contagious Equine Metritis (CEM), then clitoral swabs are often the most reliable way to find the bacteria.

The mare's reproductive tract starts with two ovaries, which lie in the abdomen near the kidneys. Eggs are released from an ovary to travel down the fallopian tube to the uterus, or womb. This is Y-shaped. At the end of the body of the uterus is the cervix. This is a sphincter which separates anything in the uterus from the outside world. It prevents infections from gaining entry into the uterus, which has relatively little defence against bacteria. During pregnancy it is, of course, the cervix which forms the restraint which helps protect the developing foal. If the cervix is opened during pregnancy, the mare may well abort. When a mare is in season, the cervix relaxes, in order to allow sperm to penetrate into the uterus if mating has occurred. Bacteria may take advantage of this also to gain entry. The final section of the female reproductive tract is the vagina, a sort of vestibule between the cervix and the lips of the vulva which are the exit to the outside world.

The male reproductive tract starts with the two testicles. These hang underneath the skin of the scrotum between the back legs. The tubes down which sperm must pass do not go directly forward from the scrotum into the penis which lies just in front, pointing towards the head. Instead they pass inwards and around the pelvis before joining the urethra. Most of the time the penis is held inside the sheath by a muscle called the cremaster muscle. When the horse is really relaxed, as for instance happens during sedation, then this muscle relaxes and allow the penis to hang downwards. It is not an abnormality for a horse to allow this to happen frequently during the day. The penis is covered by scales of a waxy substance called smegma. This is also normal. During urination and when it is sexually aroused, the penis becomes straight and hard due to the presence of extra blood which is now allowed to escape from the penile blood vessels.

The complex changes which constitute the sexual behaviour of both males and females are controlled by chemicals called hormones. A hormone is basically a substance which is released from one part of the body, for example the ovaries, in order to cause an effect in another, different, part of the body, such as the relaxation of the cervix to which I have already referred. In recent years most, if not all, the sexual hormones have been reproduced synthetically, allowing us to manipulate the reproductive cycle at will.

ABORTION

Abortion is the loss of a foetus, or developing foal, by the mare before the stage in its development when the foal can survive on its own. We usually take the normal gestation period, or length of pregnancy, to be 340 days in the horse. This is far from being a definite figure, however, because perfectly normal fully-formed foals can be born from 310-370 days. As a result it can be hard to anticipate whether a mare who starts foaling early will abort a non-viable foetus, give birth to a weak but live premature foal, or give birth to a normal foal.

Most abortions in the mare take place during the first three months of pregnancy, which is why final pregnancy diagnosis is usually left until around 100 days after the last mating with the stallion. At this time the foetus is very small, and so the owner may be unaware that the mare has aborted. As a result the mare may be said to have re-absorbed the foetus even when in fact it was expelled from her uterus.

An aborting mare follows many of the same steps as a foaling mare, in that she goes into labour, pushes out the aborted foetus and the fluids which have been around it, and then expels the foetus membranes, or afterbirth. If the abortion has been triggered off by an infection rather than some physical problem, then the foetus, fluids and membranes may all be infected with the causative organism. The most serious infectious cause of abortion is probably Equine Herpes Virus type I (EHVI). This virus is a common cause of respiratory infections in horses, but when it infects pregnant mares on the premises either by contact with the aborted material or via droplets in the air (as most respiratory infections are spread). The result may be an abortion storm, where the majority of pregnant mares abort during late pregnancy.

Action

In the UK the Thoroughbred Breeders Association has a Code of Practice which its members should follow after any known abortion. **The principal features are to have a detailed post-mortem examination carried out on the**

aborted foetus in order to try and isolate any infectious cause, and the isolation of the aborted mare so that she cannot spread an infection to any other horses. Until infections such as EHVI have been eliminated **no other horses should be moved on or off the premises,** otherwise they may spread the infection elsewhere before it has been diagnosed. The site of the abortion, whether it be out at pasture or in a stable, must be disinfected.

Some mares appear to be habitual aborters, and at one time it was suggested that this was due to a deficiency on their part of the hormone progesterone, which is the hormone that maintains pregnancy. We now know that this cannot be the case. There is no point in giving progesterone therapy during future pregnancies to mares which have aborted.

FOALING

Foaling is obviously not a disease, it is a normal occurrence, but some general guidelines on what constitutes a normal foaling may be of value in enabling the less experienced breeder to tell when something is going wrong. When this does happen, veterinary help must be summoned immediately. Mares foal normally in the vast majority of cases, but when things do go wrong, they tend to go seriously wrong because of the very strong contractions in the mare's uterus which may push things out regardless of anything else.

During the day before foaling a honey-like material may be seen oozing from the mare's nipples. This is called waxing up. It does not always occur. Some mares may have proper milk dripping from their full udders for days before they foal, with the result that the foal, when it does arrive, does not obtain any colostrum, or first milk. Most mares foal at night. They can sense when someone is watching them, and so need to be observed every minute of every hour if the foaling is to be seen. The first stage of labour lasts one to two hours. The mare may be restless, with patchy sweating over her neck and body. She may keep looking at her flank or kick at it, in fact she may show any of the symptoms of colic.

The second stage of labour is the actual delivery of the foal. As I have mentioned, this usually occurs very quickly, and this stage may take only 20 minutes from start to finish. Abdominal contractions can be seen. The mare may remain standing or lie on her side. The foal is preceded by a membrane full of fluid, which ruptures. The foal should either appear with first one front foot, then the other and finally the head, or if it is a breech, or backwards, delivery then both hind feet should appear. Any variation on these two possibilities should be viewed with concern. The rest of the foal is then pushed out. At this stage it will be joined to its mother by its umbilical cord. You should not make any attempt to cut or break this because it continues to pump blood into the foal for several minutes after birth. It ruptures either as the foal scrambles away or as the mare stands up.

The third stage of labour is the expulsion of the placental membranes. These should have been passed within 6-8 hours after the birth. At this stage also the foal should be up on its feet and suckling.

Action

Although most mares foal safely unaided, when complications do arise they occur quickly. If at all possible you should be present to monitor the foaling even if you do not need to interfere. This may involve several false alarms and wasted nights of watching.

You should obtain veterinary assistance if there is any deviation from normal. **Inexperienced breeders may consider it wise to contact their veterinary surgeon as soon as the mare starts foaling,** so that help is at hand by the time any abnormality shows itself. In any case, the mare should be checked after foaling in case her vulva has been torn. Such tears need stitching in order to prevent the airtight seal made by the vulval lips being broken. If that happens air and infection can gain entry to the vagina, and prevent the mare getting back in foal again.

Every effort should be made to ensure that the foal sucks well from its mother within 12 hours of its birth, in order to make sure that it gets enough colostrum. **The foal's navel, where the umbilical cord has severed, should be dressed with antibiotic.**

Foaling Check List
1 Have your veterinary surgeon's telephone number readily available.
2 Make sure that you have either an electrically lit foaling box, or a good torch with new batteries.
3 Have sterile catgut and antibiotic spray/powder available for treating foal's navel. Do not tie off until the cord has broken naturally.
4 Have towels available to stimulate and dry the foal if it is weak.

HEAT PERIODS AND THE OESTRUS CYCLE

As 50 per cent of horses are mares, even owners who are not interested in breeding should have some idea of the female reproductive cycle. There is a period of approximately 5 days during which the mare will be receptive to a stallion and allow herself to be mated. This is called the period of oestrus, or heat period. It is followed by a period of 16 days during which the mare will resist mating. This is called dioestrus. So the oestrus cycle last around 21 days before it starts all over again. Mares are usually only sexually active during the summer months. The Thoroughbred breeding season lasts from 15 February to 15 July, but the natural breeding season is April to August. During the winter months the ovaries of most mares are inactive, and the mare is said to be anoestrus.

The oestrus period corresponds to the time when there is a

large ripe follicle present in one of the ovaries, containing a ripe egg. During this time (usually about two thirds of the way through) the follicle will rupture and release the egg. This is called ovulation. If the mare is mated the egg will hopefully meet one of the stallion's sperm as it passes down a tube called the fallopian tube, which joins the ovary to the uterus.

During oestrus the follicle releases the female sex hormone oestrogen into the blood stream. This causes the behavioural changes which show us (and the stallion) that the mare is in oestrus. The mare may stand with her tail raised and held to one side. The muscles around her vulva may contract and relax, giving an effect rather like the winking of an eye. This may also cause the passage of frequent small amounts of urine. The mare's temperament may change markedly during oestrus. Quiet mares may become very vocal, calling to other horses. They may also become less responsive to discipline and control, which is why an awkward mare is sometimes said to be particularly 'mare-ish'. Other mares may be more placid at this time, almost mooning around after a favourite horse even if there is no stallion available.

Action

The oestrus behaviour is perfectly normal, and so needs little action in most cases. It may help to keep mares and geldings in separate groups. Some mares do not perform well during the actual time of oestrus. If this is critical, the oestrus period can be delayed by giving the mare an artificial progesterone hormone in the feed. The mare will come back into oestrus five or six days after you stop feeding the hormone. It is worth remembering that **the commonest reason for a mare stopping having oestrus periods during the summer is pregnancy.** Even when you are completely unaware that a fertile male horse has been available to the mare, you must accept that you are not there all the time. Unlike women, mares do not stop having sexual cycles after middle age.

MASTITIS

Mastitis is an infection of the mare's udder. It can be associated with a variety of bacteria, most of which gain access from the environment as a result of some slight trauma to the udder or teats. Mastitis is very rare in mares which are not suckling a foal. The first sign of mastitis is often that the mare is unwilling to let the foal suckle, and the foal accordingly starts to lose weight. The udder becomes swollen with milk as a result, and feels hot and hard. If you milk some of its secretion out with your fingers, you will see that it is changed in its consistency. Depending on the infection present, it may be watery but foul-smelling, or it may be thick and pussy. In acute cases the mare will have a raised temperature and go off her food.

Action
If both sides of the udder are affected, the first thing to do is to **bottle-feed the foal** in order to safeguard it. Antibiotic therapy may need to be given to the mare both via the blood stream and by infusion directly into the teat. **It is vital that the infected 'milk' is stripped out of the udder.** This gives relief to the mare and limits the amount of infection which can spread elsewhere. With a little practice, milking a mare is quite easy. **You should persevere until you can get no more secretion out of the teat.** In most cases modern antibiotic therapy means that the udder will return completely to normal, and the mare will be able to produce a normal amount of milk for any future foals.

RETAINED PLACENTA

As I mentioned in the section on foaling, the placenta, or after-birth, should be expelled from a mare within 6-8 hours after foaling. If it is retained, it will rapidly become infected, with severe toxic effects on the mare. Sometimes, part of the placenta can be seen hanging out of the mare's vulva, but in other cases there may be no obvious signs unless you know for certain that the placenta has not been expelled.

A mare with a retained placenta has a high temperature and appears very ill. The toxic effects of the infection may trigger off an acute laminitis. There may be a foul-smelling discharge from the vulva.

Action
After every foaling, the placenta must be checked to make sure that all of it has been passed, as even a small amount retained inside the mare can trigger off toxaemia. The placenta is Y-shaped, with each arm of the Y having a distinctly rounded end. A healthy placenta is red in colour, rather than yellowish, and has a smooth outer surface but a rough inner surface (during pregnancy it is the other way around, with the rough surface attached to the lining of the uterus, but the placenta is turned inside out as it is pushed out).

If a mare has not expelled all her placenta within 12 or so hours after foaling, contact your veterinary surgeon for advice. Sometimes the placenta may need physical removal by hand. In other cases a saline/pituitary hormone intravenous infusion will soon make the mare push it out. Whatever happens, antibiotic therapy will remove the risk from infection and toxaemia.

NEPHRITIS

Although this chapter deals with the urino-genital system, there are actually very few urinary problems in horses. Owners often suggest that their horse might have kidney problems, but these are very rare. Horses with nephritis, or inflammation of the kidneys, may lose weight. If there is pain in the kidneys, it may show as symptoms of back pain. Affected horses drink more water than normal, and pass more urine than normal, but both of these can be difficult to assess in the stable. Cloudy urine is quite normal in the horse, and is not a sign of kidney problems.

Action

If nephritis is suspected, a blood sample will soon show whether the kidneys are working normally or not. Oedema, or filling, of the legs is far more likely to be due to leg problems than kidney ones, although the treatment may involve the kidneys if diuretics are given to make the kidneys pass more urine in order to help take away the fluid.

Index

Index